CLOSING THE GAP:

UNDERSTANDING YOUR SERVICE(WO)MAN

For SIF

Yvonne Jones

Contact the author:
Yvonne.Jones@UnderstandingYourServiceman.com
www.UnderstandingYourServiceman.com

ISBN-10: 0615716687
ISBN-13: 978-0-615-71668-8

Visit us at: www.LoewenHerz-Creative.com

DEDICATION

To my fellow military families
and all those that so lovingly support them.

CONTENTS

FOREWORD

When I was growing up I had a lot of dreams. I wanted to see the world because I wished to experience what was beyond our borders. I wanted to learn how to speak English so I could understand all of the great songs that were playing on the radio. I wanted to go to college to make a better life for myself.

Indirectly, the military has given me all that, and more. Without the military, I would have never gotten to know my husband, whom I met while he was stationed in Germany. Without the military, I wouldn't have been able to see, visit, and live in so many beautiful places. Without the military, I would have never mastered the English language enough to write this book. Without the military, I would have never had the resources to actually fulfill my dreams to further my education and to be the first in my family to obtain a college degree.

The military has and still does so very much for military service(wo)men, the military family, and the military community as a whole. But it's the intangibles the military taught us that are so very significant. It's learning that no matter how difficult a challenge, with discipline, drive, and determination you can accomplish anything and are capable of so much more than you would have ever thought. It's being a part of a cause bigger and more important than yourself, and learning to say "we" instead of "me." Being a part of the military is being part of a tradition – brave Americans who fought generation after generation, from the war for independence to present-day battles in the Middle East. But most of all, it's the privilege of serving with or being amongst some of the best, bravest, and most selfless men and women you'll ever meet. It's the honor of being part of them that makes up the whole. The military instilled in us pride for our communities, but more importantly pride in ourselves. We wouldn't trade our experiences for anything. For all that the military has given and provided us, we'll be forever grateful. What we are grateful for the most, however, is our families' and friends' unconditional support and love throughout all these years. It's this affection and love for you all that motivated me to write this book.

SO YOU THINK YOU KNOW YOUR SERVICE(WO)MAN

WHY I FELT THE NEED TO WRITE THIS BOOK

According to a 2012 article found in the *New York Times*, a smaller share of Americans currently serve in the Armed Forces than at any other given point in time since World War II. This, in turn, has led to a growing gap between people in uniform and the civilian population. As the only remaining substantial connection that currently exists between the severely disconnected worlds of the military and the rest of the American society is the one found between military members and their civilian families and friends, it is imperative to strengthen this connection by promoting understanding. This book will provide you, the reader, with information needed to better comprehend your service(wo)man and his or her lifestyle.

It's not very often that we are asked to explain the differences between the military and the civilian lifestyles. This, in turn, might imply that civilians are not aware that there are distinctions between these two worlds.

While most non-military family members and friends try very hard to be supportive, most are not fully aware of what and whom they are actually supporting, as they do not truly understand our way of life.

One of the reasons for this condition is the fact that it is virtually impossible to find information that specifically relates or pertains to the relationships held between military service members and their parents, parents-in-laws, siblings, friends, or any other civilians associated with them. There are heaps of websites and books that apply to and are meant for military spouses and children, yet nothing that promotes knowledge and information pertinent to service members' other important individuals in their lives. This book is meant to remedy such an absence of resources.

It is my hope that with this book I will be able to advance and enhance the understanding of our way of life so that we, dear family and friends, are better able to understand and support each other, and rebuild bonds that might have been weakened or broken over the years.

Let me start by saying that I am not an expert on the U.S. military! I am really not the "hooah" kind of gal. I don't know most of the acronyms used within the military. To be honest, I don't even know the exact structure of our military. I have, however, been married to a serviceperson for many, many years. As such, what I do know is the life and experiences of a military spouse within a military lifestyle.

We love our non-military family members. We truly love them dearly. However, we can't deny any longer that, over the years, we have grown further and further apart. It might not have been openly stated, but our families don't really understand us and our lives any longer. And how could they? We constantly change (and are being changed) due to our experiences. After a while, it becomes easier to simply give up trying to explain your life. This, in turn, creates an ever expanding gap between civilians and the military. And, of course, our constant mobile lifestyle doesn't help this dilemma.

Unfortunately, our civilian families' and friends' limited awareness and understanding of our military lifestyle isn't just confined to our experienced hardships, such as frequent moves and deployments. Limited knowledge also contributes to the limited understanding of our personal triumphs within the military. Triumphs we feel at the end of a deployment, triumphs we feel when we receive a new assignment that our family wished for and worked toward, triumphs we experience when we advance in our careers, when we receive a good evaluation, when we are being selected for certain schools, or when we simply receive an award. However big or small those triumphs may be, they are triumphs nonetheless and can only be appropriately appreciated if their attainment is understood within its context. This is where this book comes in. This book is meant to explain our lives and illustrate our families' experiences with our everyday existence and activities within the military. With this book, I am attempting to close the gap between our non-military family members and us, members of the military community, and bring families back together again.

What is life within the military like? How is a military family currently perceived? Many people believe and express that, in one way or another, it must be quite difficult to be a military family. Agreed. This statement, however, is usually followed by stating that we surely must have known what we were getting into, back when the military was so willingly joined. This particular perception couldn't be any further from the truth.

Of course it is general knowledge that the military family will have to move around every few years. The fact that service members will have to deploy every now and then is well known, too. However, there are plenty of matters that one might not have considered simply because most don't realize how encompassing the decision of joining the military truly is. While, for instance, most realize that the military more or less controls the serving member's entire life, most do not know that this control essentially extends to the lives of the spouse and children as well. The lifestyle that comes with being in the military is an all-consuming force that does not concern itself with how any of its members might be affected by something like 6 moves in 7 years. It is a lifestyle in which every family member must sacrifice certain things to serve a purpose much larger than oneself. Even though the family unit is most important, all military families come to understand that there is a larger mission and purpose that everyone is striving toward together. But these are all concepts that are learned during the course of actually being a member of the military or part of the military community. This is knowledge and understanding acquired years after having first joined. Understanding is one thing, but it's another experience entirely to live it.

Only after having experienced multiple moves, do military families know and understand what it is like to start life afresh all over again in new places without knowing anyone. Only after having experienced multi-month-long deployments, do military families understand the challenges of being apart from each other for months at a time. And only after having lived within the military community for some time do military families know what it is like to feel isolated from, and like a stranger within the civilian world. So, while we might have had some idea about what military life would or might be like, nobody can truly comprehend until it is actually experienced.

In spite of this reality, however, many civilians continue to believe that we knew what to expect when we first associated ourselves with the military. Many believe that military life can be known without the actual experience of it. As such, we might not have the power to change how a military family's challenges are perceived and understood within the civilian world. This book, however,

is an attempt to bring our military family lifestyle a bit closer to our extended families and very own circles of friends within the civilian world so as to bring civilian and military families back together again.
Let's get reacquainted.

Having covered why I felt the need to write this book, I'd now like to explain the choice of this book's title *Closing The Gap: Understanding Your Service(wo)man.* Substituting 'Service(wo)man" with the word 'Soldier" would have been more catchy. However, I want this book to appeal and apply to all families and friends of our service(wo)men of every single branch within our military. Many believe that the term 'Soldier" is a general term used for anyone wearing the uniform. This definition might hold true with its looser usage within the civilian world, but is considered inaccurate in the military.

There are individual designations of each branch of service. Here is a quick overview:

MILITARY BRANCH		SERVING INDIVIDUAL	
ARMY	-	Soldier	
MARINE	-	Marine	Serviceperson/
AIR FORCE	-	Airman	Service(wo)man
NAVY	-	Sailor	
COAST GUARD	-	Coast Guardsman	

The politically correct term for a cross-branch collective or generic reference to the members of any given branch is *"Serviceperson"* or *"Serviceman,"* hence, the title. Therefore, whether your *"Service(wo)man"* is in the Army, Marine Corps, Navy, Air Force, or Coast Guard, this book will apply to you!

Before we move on to the next part of this chapter, I would like to present the following questions in order to see how much you currently know about your service(wo)man and their lifestyle.

HOW MUCH DO YOU KNOW ABOUT YOUR SERVICE(WO)MAN'S MILITARY LIFE?
1. What is the official name of the military installation your service(wo)man is currently stationed at?
2. What is your service(wo)man's current job title and what are some of the assigned job responsibilities?
3. Does your service(wo)man plan on retiring within the military? If so, how much longer does your service(wo)man have to serve until retirement?
4. Of all the installations your service(wo)man has been assigned to so far, which one is her/his favorite, and why?
5. When was your service(wo)man last deployed, and what was the location?
6. What does your service(wo)man value about the military life?
7. Why did your service(wo)man join the military?
8. How long has your service(wo)man been part of the military now?

We get it! These somewhat specific facts about your service(wo)man's life might not be the most interesting or most exciting information to know or even to retain. However, knowing or not knowing the answers to those questions may be a good indicator of how well you have been able to keep up with your service(wo)man's evolving and ever-changing military career and the lifestyle it brings with it.

Knowing very little about your service(wo)man's lifestyle, in fact, may result in a somewhat vicious cycle that it will get harder to escape from as time goes on: You might feel a bit embarrassed that you don't know more about his or her life, but believe that you ought to know more. And because of this very belief that you ought to know more, you have now become hesitant or too embarrassed to ask. As a result, you either pretend to know and understand, or avoid military-related subjects altogether.

This is where this book comes in. Don't believe for a minute that it is ever too late to ask us about our military lives. We'd rather have you ask us late, than never. By asking, you show that you are interested in our lives. And your expressed interest, in turn, shows your support. And support is the greatest gift you can extend to your service(wo)man.

Rebuilding your relationship and getting closer by learning more about your service member will take some time and may require some work. By taking the time to learn as much as possible about your service(wo)man's life and military lifestyle, however, you'll be able to gradually alleviate the gap that might have formed itself between the two of you over the years.

While this gap may not exist among all the readers and their service(wo)men, educating yourself will still benefit you in that this new knowledge and understanding enables you to strengthen your relationship with your military member. You have demonstrated that you care deeply simply by reading this book. Please know that we are so very thankful and couldn't do any of what we do without you.

WHO THIS BOOK IS FOR

Who specifically is this book for? The book will be most useful to people in one of the four categories below:

I.	**Parents and siblings** (Parents and siblings whose child/sibling is in the military)
II.	**In-laws** (Parents of the husband/wife married to the military person)
III.	**Friends** of military personnel who seek to understand their friends' life/lifestyle
IV.	**Other interested individuals**

As a member of either one of those groups, have you ever noticed that, when trying to find information regarding your service(wo)man that relates and/or pertains specifically to your circumstance, documentation is virtually nonexistent? Have you ever tried to find a particular piece of information about the lifestyle of your service(wo)man, only to find that there are websites and books that mostly apply to and are meant for military spouses and children, but not for you as a parent, sibling, or friend of a military member? It seems that there aren't any real resources out there specifically for military parents, in-laws, or friends to help them understand what their loved one is going through. Why is there such an absence of resources? Is it because you don't need or don't want to know such information? The mere fact that you sought out, found, and are currently reading this book is evidence to the contrary.

In order to stay close to your service(wo)man and to his or her family, you need to be able to understand their lives, as it is quite different from any civilian life. This book won't provide you with a crash course on military terminology, abbreviations, or the basic setup of rank and structure within the different branches of the military; you can find this type of information with ease on the Internet. What this book will provide you with, however, is the information you will need in order to better understand your service(wo)man's lifestyle, which in turn will enable you to provide physical and emotional support to your loved ones and rebuild your relationship with them. I truly believe that explaining and teaching civilians like yourself about the military community and our way of life will benefit us all. We certainly don't expect outsiders to truly understand us, but it sure would be nice if the civilians closest to us, such as our parents or siblings, could learn to understand our lives a little bit better.

WHAT THIS BOOK IS NOT

This book is
   NOT meant to be a private account of our lives.
   NOT meant to justify and explain the existence and mission of the military.
   NOT meant to explain terminology, abbreviations, or structures used within the military.
   NOT meant to be a deployment or reintegration guide.
   NOT meant to be a guide on how to cope with loss.
   NOT meant to complain about the military and/or the lifestyle that comes with it.

For those items mentioned above, there are plenty of other books, websites, and blogs out there that do a wonderful and important job covering and explaining these topics and issues.

I'd also like to point out that this book won't distinguish between officers and enlisted, as it is meant to apply to all service members within the military. Instead of going into specifics and technical details, I've kept most topics broad, because the aim of this book is to provide an overview of the most important and most influential elements within our military lives.

I felt it necessary to include this sort of disclaimer in order to prevent the reader from developing false expectations of this book. Again, *Closing the Gap: Understanding Your Service(wo)man* was written purely in order to help the non-veteran or non-military family member or friend understand loved ones and their lives a little bit better so as to help them reform bonds that may have become strained with their loved ones in the military.

I would like to dedicate selected sections of *Closing the Gap: Understanding Your Service(wo)man* to very special individuals I was fortunate enough to meet during our journey within the military. No matter how brief our actual encounter, these people truly touched my heart. Sometimes it is those from whom you'd least expect it that have the most defining impact on your life...

2

WHO WE ARE – WHO YOU ARE

WHO WE ARE
"MILITARY FAMILY"

In order to explain to you what a military family is, let's look at the applicable creed and motto your service(wo)man is encouraged to live by.

Due to its prominent use in different forms of entertainment, such as movies and songs, the Rifleman's Creed is often mistakenly thought to be the creed of all military branches. Each branch within the military, however, has its own creed, which are depicted below.

CLOSING THE GAP: UNDERSTANDING YOUR SERVICE(WO)MAN

ARMY U.S. SOLDIER'S CREED:	AIRFORCE THE AIRMAN'S CREED:
I am an American Soldier. I am a Warrior and a member of a team. I serve the people of the United States, and live the Army Values. I will always place the mission first. I will never accept defeat. I will never quit. I will never leave a fallen comrade. I am disciplined, physically and mentally tough, trained and proficient in my warrior tasks and drills. I always maintain my arms, my equipment and myself. I am an expert and I am a professional. I stand ready to deploy, engage, and destroy the enemies of the United States of America in close combat. I am a guardian of freedom and the American way of life. I am an American Soldier.	I am an American Airman. I am a Warrior. I have answered my Nation's call. I am an American Airman. My mission is to Fly, Fight, and Win. I am faithful to a Proud Heritage, A Tradition of Honor, And a Legacy of Valor. I am an American Airman. Guardian of Freedom and Justice, My Nation's Sword and Shield, Its Sentry and Avenger. I defend my Country with my Life. I am an American Airman. Wingman, Leader, Warrior. I will never leave an Airman behind. I will never falter, And I will not fail.

COAST GUARD CREED OF THE U.S. COAST GUARDSMAN:	MARINE RIFLEMAN'S CREED:
I am proud to be a United States Coast Guardsman.	This is my rifle. There are many like it, but this one is mine.
I revere that long line of expert seamen who by their devotion to duty and sacrifice of self have made it possible for me to be a member of a service honored and respected, in peace and in war, throughout the world.	My rifle is my best friend. It is my life. I must master it as I must master my life. My rifle, without me, is useless. Without my rifle, I am useless. I must fire my rifle true. I must shoot straighter than my enemy
I never, by word or deed, will bring reproach upon the fair name of my service, nor permit others to do so unchallenged.	who is trying to kill me. I must shoot him before he shoots me. I will...
I will cheerfully and willingly obey all lawful orders.	My rifle and myself know that what counts in this war is not the rounds we fire, the noise of our
I will always be on time to relieve, and shall endeavor to do more, rather than less, than my share.	burst, or the smoke we make. We know that it is the hits that count. We will hit...
I will always be at my station, alert and attending to my duties.	My rifle is human, even as I, because it is my life. Thus, I will learn it as a brother. I will learn its
I shall, so far as I am able, bring to my seniors solutions, not problems.	weaknesses, its strength, its parts, its accessories, its sights and its barrel.
I shall live joyously, but always with due regard for the rights and privileges of others.	I will keep my rifle clean and ready, even as I am clean and ready. We will become part of each other. We will...
I shall endeavor to be a model citizen in the community in which I live.	Before God, I swear this creed. My rifle and myself are the defenders of my country. We are the masters
I shall sell life dearly to an enemy of my country, but give it freely to rescue those in peril.	of our enemy. We are the saviors of my life.
With God's help, I shall endeavor to be one of His noblest Works... A UNITED STATES COAST GUARDSMAN.	So be it, until victory is America's and there is no enemy, but peace!

NAVY SAILOR'S CREED:	MOTTOS ARMED FORCES:
I am a United States Sailor. I will support and defend the Constitution of the United States of America and I will obey the orders of those appointed over me. I represent the fighting spirit of the Navy and those who have gone before me to defend freedom and democracy around the world. I proudly serve my country's Navy combat team with Honor, Courage and Commitment. I am committed to excellence and the fair treatment of all.	ARMY "This We'll Defend" AIRFORCE "Aim High ... Fly-Fight-Win" COAST GUARD "Semper Paratus" (Always Ready) MARINE "Semper Fidelis" (Always Faithful) NAVY "Non Sibi Sed Patriae" (Not For Self But For Country)

Those creeds and mottos reflect the pride, beliefs, and top priorities of your service(wo)man. Those beliefs, are the driving force that keep your service(wo)man going during inspirational acts of bravery and sacrifice, during periods of long separations, danger and fear of injury and loss. Military service penetrates and influences the entire family to an extent unmatched by civilian employment. Military life is hard to describe, but ultimately, it is a "way of life" as opposed to a job or a career. Military life is not an easy life, and is most certainly not for everyone. But most of us wouldn't want to change who and what we are. We travel all over the world and meet some truly amazing people along the way with whom we create lifelong, lasting friendships. But who are "we"?

A military family, by definition, is a unit that usually consists of a husband and wife and children, with either the husband and/or wife as the primary military member.[1] Military families try to help and support each other through family readiness and support groups, with the aim of empowering and comforting family members by providing important knowledge and information, as well as a place to meet with others that go through the same worries, anxieties, and experiences that civilian friends can't easily relate to or understand. There is a certain sense of comfort and strength in knowing that most people surrounding us have similar life experiences, similar values, and similar expectations.

We currently live in a culture where less than one percent of the U.S. population meets the definition of being military personnel.[2] Less than one percent! Here is a visual representation of the number of Americans serving in the military.

U.S. POPULATION

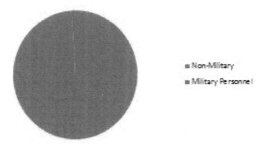

Let's try to put this information into perspective. With a rate of service that is less than one percent of the entire population, for every service(wo)man within the United States Military, there are about 107 civilians. Looking at it from yet another perspective, there are about 18,000 professional athletes within the U.S., meaning that we only have about 160 times more individuals protecting and defending the United States (and its interests) than there are individuals that are paid to play sports to entertain us. As you can see, not many share your experiences and challenges of being a military parent, sibling, in-law, or simply a friend.

WHO YOU ARE
(In Relation To The "Military Family")

I. MILITARY PARENTS & SIBLINGS

As a parent or a sibling of a service(wo)man, you more or less will have to (or already do) support his or her decision to join the military if you want to remain a tightly knit family unit. However, civilians like yourself are often unfamiliar with our military lifestyles and what is expected of us. While we, the military family, are usually surrounded by other like-minded individuals within our military community, you as military parents or siblings might not have such an understanding support network, simply because most of your friends and neighbors don't have a service(wo)man in their lives. At times, you might feel alone in this regard, as none, or very few, of your friends have sons, daughters, brothers, or sisters that currently serve the military and truly understand what they and you are going through at certain periods, such as worry and concern during your loved one's deployment.

All parents miss their children at one point or another, no matter how old or far away they are. But your situation differs in that you might not only feel a geographical distance, but also an increasing sense of emotional separation due to the two different worlds we, the military family, and you, our military parents and siblings, live in.

Despite those differences, please know and be assured that we love and miss you dearly. We might not tell you this often enough, but we, too, wish that we could just "swing by" your place to have a nice family dinner together. We, too, yearn to spend holidays with you without having to drive or fly for hours to reach you. And we, too, would like to be able to simply call you whenever it pops into our minds without having to consider time zone differences.

But no matter how far we are from you geographically, we'll always love you. Thank you for reading this book!

II. MILITARY IN-LAWS

Your daughter or son is married to a military service member. Otherwise however, your family may not be affiliated with the military. As such, your knowledge about the military and the way of life it brings with it may be limited. You do, however, desire to learn and understand more in order to remain close to your child and his or her family.

You may face many of the same challenges a military parent will come across. I won't lie. It will be hard at times as this new way of life might cause your child having to move every so often, thereby being far away from you geographically. But while this way of life might be difficult and different at times, please remember that it will also provide your child's family with so many beautiful and rewarding opportunities, experiences and choices. But most importantly, by being married to a military member, your son or your daughter is supporting a cause he or she believes in.

Sometimes we might forget that our affiliation with the military also inevitably affects most of our other close family members. Thank you for taking the time to learn more! Thank you for loving us the way you do!

III. FRIENDS OF THE "MILITARY FAMILY"
- For Melissa -

As previously stated, with serving nationals making up less than one percent of the entire population of the United States, for every service(wo)man within the United States Military, there are about 107 civilians.

Consequently, chances of us as military family members interacting with and befriending civilians are quite high, at least when seen from our perspective. For the majority of civilians, on the other hand, it is quite unusual to befriend military family members, mainly because there aren't very many around, as they are rather concentrated and clustered around military installations. And if there are, they won't stay for very long.

There are two time periods we might have or will meet you in: (a) before we joined or became affiliated with the military, or (b) during our military lives. As is to be expected, we hold far more friends from category (a) within the civilian world, than we do from category (b). But no matter when we met, certain things might have changed due to the fact that the military is a large part of our lives now.

For instance, your military friends will not be able to remain stationary. That is, they will have to move every other year or so. It is understandably frustrating for you to constantly having to update our addresses and to keep track of us. It also doesn't help that, sometimes for years at a time, you aren't quite sure where exactly we currently reside; you may not even know what country! This, among other things, can make friendships challenging, since the only contact you may have at times is via phone or the internet. Maintaining "long-distance" friendships takes lots of effort in order to stay and feel connected. Just remember that, while we might not be close geographically, you still remain very close to our hearts.

It's all too easy to drift apart from your military friends, but please don't give up on us! We greatly value our friendships within a more stationary world. While I'm aware that we can't expect you to fully understand our way of life, I do hope that through the insights within this book, we will be able to bridge this gap between our worlds so that you can remain close to your military friends.

Unless you grew up with us, you might not know a whole lot about our personal lives. We'll always be the new people on your block or in your town. We'll always be those that won't quite fit into your circle of friendships that you had time to establish and work on over many, many years. But that doesn't mean we can't be true friends, right? We love to learn about each and every one of you. We greatly enjoy our conversations and the small bonds that we might share with each other.

Every time we move again, we fear anew that these friendships we have grown so very fond of will eventually dissolve like so many others have in the past when we moved to a new duty station. Every single time we move to a new place, we put ourselves out there again, seeking new friendships within the civilian world. It's hard. And it gets harder with each additional move. Sometimes, our worlds seem so very far apart. But how can two groups of people, separated by a canyon of experience, come together? They both begin to build a bridge that extends from their side to the other so that they can meet in the middle. The very fact that you picked up this book and are willing to read it shows that you are willing to build that bridge. What a great friend you are. Thank you!

Not much information is currently available that tries to explain the military's way of life to our military parents, civilian family members, or civilian friends. You are very important to us. We truly want to keep you in our lives. In an effort to do so, I wrote this book, because I believe that knowledge indeed is power – power to bring us closer together. Thank you for loving us!

What follows are some of the most important subject areas within a military life.

In Chapter 3, you will find enlightenment and an explanation on the process of assignments, as assignments mark the beginning of every prospective relocation of our families;

Chapter 4 will cover the actual relocation and everything else it entails;

Chapter 5 discusses the military culture;

Chapter 6 analyzes and explains what it is like for military families to go through each and everyone's dreaded deployment and the process it involves, and, finally;

In Chapter 7 you will find a brief summary of the differences found between the civilian and military worlds. The majority of the chapters are followed by the most common misconceptions of each of these topics.

3

WHERE TO NEXT? ASSIGNMENTS

Assignments are a period of great anxiety within military families. It's not simply a process of picking and receiving what one chose or wished for. This process involves a lot more than that.

Usually, your loved one in the military will simply tell you that the next move is very imminent. And before you know it, you are informed of where he or she is moving to next. But how in the world did your service(wo)man decide where to go next? Or did s/he get to decide at all? While the assignment process is a very complicated one, I would like to focus only on the main factors that influence the process in order to give you a small glimpse of how, why, and when we receive the assignments we do.

The assignment process is based on several factors and considerations. In general, the duty station selection is based upon four elements: 1) Military Requirements, 2) Availability for Assignment, 3) Career Development Needs, and 4) Preferences.[3]

In the most general terms, "Military Requirements" are those vacant positions that must be filled, also called "Needs of the Military." "Availability for Assignment" means that a serviceperson has completed the previously specified tour length, and is therefore eligible to be reassigned again.

The consideration of a military member's "Career Development Needs" is very important. Each branch and functional area within the military has its own life cycle development model. Your service(wo)man's career needs are examined in light of these models in order to ensure the next assignment is progressive, sequential and achieves certain career development goals.

Besides "Military Requirements," "Availability," and "Career Development Needs," those responsible for (re)assignments also look at other considerations when arriving at appropriate assignments for personnel, such as a service(wo)man's "Preferences." Assignment managers may not be able to satisfy all preferences because of other previously discussed requirements, but they do attempt to satisfy as many as possible.

A military family's preferences may be based on a number of elements, two of them being the new duty station's location and the actual job the service member will be required to perform. Some military families emphasize the importance of *where* they are going to live for the next couple of years, while others base their decisions upon the *kind of work* the service(wo)man will get to do.

In most cases, the service(wo)man is given choices, and we are able to pick from a number of preselected assignment options, and then rank those according to the family unit's preferences. But again, while these preferences might be considered, the overriding deciding factor is where your service(wo)man is needed the most. If this decision coincides with one of the military family's preferences, great. If not, we are simply assigned to where the military wants us, regardless.

Now that you have some idea how the (re)assignment process works, let's look at some possible duty locations your service(wo)man might be assigned to. Below is a map which depicts the states and nations of some major and minor United States military installations.

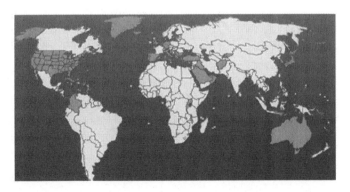

As you can see, the military has a number of overseas duty locations, such as in Europe or Japan. These are usually considered standard overseas tours, which allow the service(wo)man to elect to bring his or her family along for the duration of the assignment. Some other overseas duty locations, however (like most assignments to Korea), are considered to be remote overseas tours, which means that one's family cannot be brought along. Those remote overseas tours are usually set for 12-month periods. While those 12 months usually mean a year-long separation from one's family unit and loved ones like yourself, military personnel returning from remote tours are usually given assignment preference over those returning from a standard tour. Therefore, if a military family desires a very specific (and usually popular) duty location but knows that this will be difficult to obtain, they could volunteer for a remote overseas tour. After those 12 months, then, the military family's chances of receiving their desired duty location are much higher, but not guaranteed. This, indeed, can be a very tricky (if not dangerous) "game."

Of course, if there are not enough volunteers for overseas vacancies, service(wo)men can be involuntarily assigned overseas as well.

As you can see, the assignment of your loved one's new duty station is not always that clear cut and involves the consideration of multiple factors. Moreover, as military members increase in rank, the assignment process becomes even more difficult because the list of possible jobs grows smaller and smaller.

The assignment period is usually a very exciting, but also very nerve-racking time for the entire military family. This is a time where mental support from friends and extended family is greatly welcomed and appreciated, as this phase of life is full of uncertainty and requires a lot of patience. We usually can barely wait to find out where we're going next, simply because it ends months of guessing and painful ambiguity.

But finding out about our next assignment also indicates the end of our time at our current duty station, starting a phase of yet another set of goodbyes and painful separations. And that's what the next chapter is meant to address and focus on: the moving process.

MAIN MISCONCEPTIONS REGARDING ASSIGNMENTS

WRONG: Spouses and children are not affected by the military.

TRUE: The military is all-consuming in that it not only forces the serving member to become completely involved in every aspect of the military, but it also pulls in the spouse and children. It is a lifestyle in which every family member has to sacrifice certain things to serve a larger good.

WRONG: We don't miss our civilian families and friends.

TRUE: We miss our families and friends dearly, as you are very important to us.

WRONG: We decide when and where to move next.

TRUE: An assignment officer or career manager decides when and where we'll move to next.

WRONG: The assignment process is quick and painless, and once a decision has been made, it will not and cannot be changed.

TRUE: The assignment process usually takes months. Within the military, nothing is set in stone. Everything can change at a moment's notice.

WRONG: We don't need anyone's support, since we're simply used to this type of lifestyle.

TRUE: During the assignment period, we very much need your emotional support, as this phase involves a lot of uncertainty and requires a lot of patience.

WRONG: Phrases like "Well, that's the military life for you," or "Been there, done that," will help us feel better and understood.

TRUE: What we want and really need every so often are words of support, sympathy, and even commiseration at times. Statements like those mentioned above just show that we haven't truly been heard or that we haven't truly been understood. Those words, that were meant to make us feel better, just seem to belittle our feelings that we've just openly expressed. Sometimes it's best to simply listen and acknowledge the other person's feelings.

4

MOVE
- For Barb -

This chapter I would like to entirely dedicate to the subject of moving, as in the process of relocating from one place of residency to another. Moving impacts our lives greatly, and is therefore an important topic to address when explaining the military lifestyle to you.

"Home is where the Military sends us," is a well-known phrase within the military community. And it really does seem to be true. Well, it has to be! Military families often move to cities they've never visited before. Thus, in order to feel some sort of connection to a new place, we simply have to accept that this new locale will be our home for a while. Acceptance makes everything much easier and a lot more enjoyable. When military family members are asked where their home is, they often have difficulty finding an appropriate answer. Where and what really is a home? It can be a place of birth, where one grew up, where one lived the longest, or where one lives now. So while *you* associate the word "home" with one particular town, we must or have come to terms with the fact that the place we call home changes every so often.

Few things in life match the stress and strain of a big

move.   Nearly 40 million Americans move each year, including more than half a million active military personnel.[4] The typical military family moves every three years, but many relocate every 2 years or even every year. Now let's try the following thought-experiment:

Have you moved from one city to another before? If you have, try to recall your last big move, meaning from one town or city to another. Remember how stressed you were? Remember how worried you were that you might forget something or that something valuable might break during the move? Remember how sad you were, having to leave all your friends and family behind? Remember how hard it was trying to sell your house? Remember how frustrating it was, having to find a new place to live, having to set up your utilities once more, and having to find a new reliable babysitter for your kids? Sometimes it's hard to remember those demanding and challenging times, mainly because our brain prefers to remember the more pleasant and enjoyable moments in life. Nevertheless, try to recall how much pressure and anxiety you felt during your move. And now try to imagine having to do this every 2 to 3 years.

Sure, excitement may play a big part as well. After all, who doesn't get excited about a fresh start with a new job that you have been working toward, or a beautiful new house you have been dreaming and hoping for? While all this has still retained some sort of excitement for us as well, leaving family and friends behind every other year does get more and more demanding and tiring over time.

For most military families, moving is an inevitable and frequent part of life.[5] Contrary to popular beliefs, however, it does NOT get easier over time! And the fact that every family within the military has to go through similar changes does NOT soften the impact on each individual family either.

What may get easier for some military families is the organizational part of a move itself, but the actual mental process within each one of us does not. And while grownups may have found a more or less agreeable way to cope with separation from the known and familiar, our little ones may have not. Our children, especially the young ones, don't understand why we have to prepare for yet another move, why they have to say goodbye to all their new friends again, and why they have to get accustomed to yet another babysitter.

Like many other military family members, I find myself resigned to numbness, indifference and emotionlessness. These are just a few of the emotional states I experience during the actual moving process. Before every move I find myself trying to heartlessly find something wrong with the current place; be it the house, the people around us, or the entire town. This place simply has to be bad, because this very belief makes leaving it behind seemingly easier and less painful.

Have you ever said goodbye, in tears, while the other side seemed emotionless, or even cold? While you were sobbing and crying, devastated at the loss of their company, this other person somehow managed to appear untouched by the farewell. This sort of departure appears to be very common when military family members say their goodbyes to loved ones and new friends. Why is that? Are we just a heartless breed?

Don't be fooled by our outer emotionless and tough appearance! While our exterior might seem solid and composed, it is really just a façade that created itself over time. A façade as an outcome of natural self-preservation, meant to shield us from the pain of harsh circumstances and goodbyes when having to move every 2-3 years.

While such a façade may appear as rejection, as if we never cared to begin with, I assure and promise you that all we are waiting for during these times is an understanding hug and an acknowledging voice. Don't let yourself be discouraged to approach us, but rather know that we do care, even if it's not always visible from the outside.

Now that we have covered the move in general, let's look at a graph that illustrates what a regular moving process as a military family entails. We have already discussed the assignment process, so here I will go over and explain the other steps that come after the assignment.

PCS ORDERS

Once we've made it through yet another period of painful uncertainty during the assignment process (described in the previous chapter), we now have to wait for orders. Your service(wo)man's set of orders is the paperwork that makes the projected move official. The Permanent Change of Station (PCS) orders generally signal the authorized go-ahead to officially begin organizing for relocation.

(Side Note: We usually can't prepare too far ahead for the move, as plans can always change from one minute to the next within the military. It is very common to receive a phone call a month or so prior to the planned move in which we are informed that the next duty station has been changed. So when preparing ourselves for relocation to Alaska, we may be notified of new relocation orders to Florida.)

OUTPROCESSING

Before permanently leaving a duty station, your service(wo)man will be required to out-process. Out-processing means to "withdraw" or "deregister" from numerous agencies, businesses, and offices; but the process can't begin until official orders have been received. During out-processing, the packing, loading, and transportation of our household goods will have to be set up and coordinated. This is also the time during which your service(wo)man is generally required to attend numerous briefings to adequately prepare for each relocation. The military provides offices to assist families with the moving process, which, thankfully, reduces some of the burden on the families.

THE ACTUAL MOVE

For a PCS move, we are generally given three choices of how to transport our belongings: (1) commercial movers hired by the military, (2) a DITY (Do-IT-Yourself) move, or (3) a partial DITY move (a combination of commercial movers and DITY). The military pays for the move of our belongings for relocation. The cost is usually based on the estimated weight of the household items, which is not to exceed a predetermined weight allowance. The military will usually pay an additional allowance to help offset the costs of canceling and restarting necessities such as utilities, cable, and phone.

If the service(wo)man decides to go with a commercial mover, the military hires a professional contractor to pack and move all household goods. On the actual moving day, movers come to wrap and pack everything up. If things get broken, they usually get replaced. Paperwork on damaged or missing items will have to be filed by specific deadlines. Those broken items, then, will have to be held onto until the claims office has replaced them through the claims process.

CLEANING

Once the movers load the last box onto their truck and take off with our belongings, the cleaning process begins. Government housing is considered one of the benefits of military life, but anyone who has lived on post can testify that this boon can sometimes be a bane. PCS time is a good example. As if moving isn't stressful enough, clearing quarters can add one more headache to a military family's life. When I say clean the house, I'm not talking about vacuuming the carpet, mowing the lawn, and dusting the vents. A military cleaning is just what it sounds like: a MILITARY standard of cleaning.[6]

ARRIVING ON THE OTHER END: THE NEW PLACE

We finally make it to our "temporarily final" destination – our new duty station. What next? Depending on the military installation, military families can chose to either live on post in the provided military housing, or off post in rented or purchased properties. Because of the very fact that we move so frequently, military families tend to live in base housing or in rental properties.

Housing within military installations is quite comparable to small cities that have their very own shopping, dining, sports and entertainment facilities, as well as their own chapels. Within these self-contained worlds, military culture is primary, and the culture found outside the military installation is secondary. Pervaded by military norms and expectations, life within a military installation is quite different from civilian culture.

While some service(wo)man may be able to receive base housing right away, many others find themselves on long waiting lists that can range from months to years. Waiting for military quarters can indeed postpone getting settled into the new community, as it marks yet another period of waiting with frustrating delays.

Living in base housing or in off-base rentals usually brings another set of challenges with it that you usually wouldn't think about or consider to be a big issue.

Let's look at something as simple as plain, white walls. To you, this might not seem like a very big deal, but seemingly unimportant things like restrictions on the way you may or may not be able to decorate your home are just another reminder that you aren't truly home.

Finally, there is the challenge of switching from single-family homes in low-cost areas to apartments or townhomes in high-cost areas. This usually means either downsizing by permanently parting with some of our furniture, or temporarily storing these items. Either way, having to constantly change one's furniture inventory can intensify the feeling of displacement and not being home.

OVERSEAS MOVES

Most overseas locations are "weight restricted" destinations, which means that we are only allowed to ship a portion of our PCS weight allowance.[7] Deciding what to pack, what to ship, and what to store can be a real challenge when moving overseas.

When moving overseas, the transportation of household goods can take a long time. At such times, military families may have to live without most of their belongings for two or three months at a time while those items are in transit. Again, this might not seem like a big deal, but trying to be without your kids' toys, sleeping on air mattresses, and living in a completely empty house or apartment without any furniture for weeks and months at a time can be a difficult challenge, indeed. For that reason, some military installations provide "loaner" furniture to assist with this transition.

Another challenge of moving overseas is the notorious culture shock, which comes sooner for some than for others. Visiting a new country with its unique culture, customs, and traditions is one thing; but living there permanently is quite another. To overcome and alleviate this initial shock of moving overseas, we usually try to acclimate ourselves to the customs and cultures of the foreign country we now call our home for the next couple of years by attending overseas briefings. "When in Rome, do as the Romans do" is a proverb that, when respected and applied, usually serves us very well during those assignments abroad.

RECONNECTING SOCIALLY

A couple of weeks after the move, when stress has finally begun to dissolve and settle, life begins to return to a sense of normalcy. I write "sense of normalcy" because life doesn't simply RETURN to normalcy, but BECOMES normal again by acclimating and establishing new routines. It's a NEW normal. And that is usually the time when the realization hits that once again we have to start over.
New questions pop into our heads: Will we be able to make new friends? Will the kids be able to integrate smoothly? How hard will it be and how long will it take this time to reintegrate?

For family members, one of the toughest parts of military life has to be making new friends, only to have the military take them away again. We've frequently felt so sick and tired of moving so often that we considered that it would be easier to just give up on making new friends all together. But what would that really mean? Do we really want to isolate ourselves? Making friends might be tough, but we keep reminding ourselves that new friendships can help us find our own comfort in a new community that will be our home for the next months to come.

But what types of friends are we really talking about? Acquaintances? Companions? Or truly deep running friendships? How long does it normally take a person to form new friendships? How long does it take to feel comfortable enough with someone new to be able to call this person a good and close friend; a friend that you can talk to about anything; a friend you can confide in and reveal your innermost feelings to; a friend you can simply open your heart to? A couple of months, years even? Sadly, we don't have time to form these types of close friendships. Or maybe it's just me. It takes me quite a while to feel relaxed enough around somebody to truly talk about myself. It usually takes me a couple of months, and by the time I finally feel comfortable, either my family has to move again, or our friends have to PCS. Unless we are lucky enough to meet those people early on within our new assignment, and unless our assignment periods somewhat coincide with each other (meaning they get to the same duty station around the same time we do), friendships don't really have enough time to prosper and thrive.

However, military life does change people. As such, I have met plenty of people over the years, who have learned to open up quickly and more easily, which in turn helps to quickly establish and maintain new friendships.

After 13 years of being a military wife, I have learned to appreciate and accept the diversity of friendships in my life. As I stopped comparing them to the past and stopped judging them for what I thought they could or ought to be, I was able to redefine my belief and understanding of the meaning of friendship. All are valuable in their own ways, and should be treated and appreciated as such. Sure, not all friendships are easy. Some require real effort. But once we realize this fact to be true, we'll be able to learn to be patient with and more understanding of one another.

Saying goodbye to friends is hard; but we try to take comfort in knowing that our paths might cross again. Sometimes we are lucky enough to bump into them again somewhere down the road.

The bright side of it all is just that - we have friends scattered all over the world! Wherever we go in the future, we won't be far from at least a friend or two. Our moves will reunite us with old friends while leading us to new friendships along the way.[8]

WHAT WE WISH FOR

While we do value the military life and all the opportunities it provides, we can't wait to finally be able to pick a place we can truly call home. A place we know we'll remain for a very long time. A place where we can plant flowers, vegetables, and other plants whose fruits we will be able to enjoy because we'll finally stay long enough to eat the ripened products. A place we can buy specific pieces of furniture for, because we bought it for this very specific spot within this very specific house. A beautiful piece of furniture that we know for certain won't get broken or damaged in the next move, because there won't be one. We look forward to a home with no expiration date attached to it.

We can't wait to meet our new neighbors, knowing that we will live door to door for a long time to come. We can't wait to feel ourselves opening up to the people around us because we know we won't have to say goodbye any time soon. We can't wait to become really familiar with the local grocery store where we will be able to remember what products we can find in which aisle, simply because we will have had the chance to shop there for a long, long time. We can't wait to finally be able to drill holes into a wall, because we don't have to worry about having to patch it up again in a couple of months so that the housing inspector will return our deposit and clear our papers. We can't wait to unpack EVERYTHING, knowing that we won't have to repack any time soon.

More than once have I heard, "Well, if you crave to settle, then just settle. Who can stop you?" But things aren't always as simple as they seem. There are indeed some facts most people don't know about or forget to consider. Being in the military is associated with a certain service commitment, a period of obligated military service. For example, if you become an Air Force pilot, you have to agree to an active service commitment of 10 years following pilot training. Air Force pilot training is very expensive, and the Air Force simply wants to make sure they get their investment back. It may surprise you to learn that everyone who joins the military for the first time incurs a MINIMUM eight year service commitment. That's right, EIGHT years! It doesn't matter if you signed a two year active duty contract, a four year contract, or even a six year contract. Your total military commitment is eight years. Whatever amount of time not spent on active duty must be served within a Reserve component.[9]

Any time certain promotions have been accepted, the service(wo)man incurs an additional active service obligation (ADSO). Reassignment to and from an overseas location creates an extra ADSO. The attendance of any military courses or fully funded courses at civilian institutions of 60 days or more also incurs an ADSO.[10] I could go on and on listing all those actions that incur additional ADSOs. Sure, we always have a choice. But after having invested eight full years of your life in something or someone, how easy would it really be for anyone to just turn around and walk away? Consecutive obligations add up quickly, bringing us closer to the rewards in the end, an early retirement, which will be a nice supplement to whatever we decide to do in the future. And once we've hit the 10-year halfway mark, it's usually more beneficial to stay in until retirement altogether.

As you can see, we can't just pack our stuff and leave whenever we feel like it. True, the initial sign up was very intentional. And yes, when we first associated ourselves with the military and its lifestyle, we knew to some extent that it was going to be different and difficult at times. But military or not, we are still human and feel the same pain that any type of separation during a move brings with it.

The grass is always greener on the other side. People who never really leave their hometown might seek a lifestyle similar to ours, in which they get to see the world, get to experience different cultures and sceneries, and get the chance to experience some sort of adventure. But while this sort of lifestyle is interesting, I can't wait to finally find a place that I can call my home. Until then, I remind myself that the most precious possessions I'll take with me on every move aren't packed up in boxes. They can't be broken by the movers or lost somewhere between state lines. My most precious possessions are the memories. My memories. For now, home is where the military sends us, as long as I am with my significant other.

What follows is a wonderful article I found on *thecreativemama.com*, written by a military spouse. This positively written post sheds some light on how hard these transitions are at times. The author, Stephanie Cribbs Beaty, has graciously given her permission to reprint.

A Day In The Life of a Military Move
By Stephanie Cribbs Beaty

It's still dark outside on Saturday morning. The alarm on my phone buzzes, signaling the beginning of the day. 3:30 AM. We are scheduled to arrive at the Space A (space available) military terminal at 4:30 for check-in with a 6:30 AM takeoff to Jacksonville, Fla.

By spring, our orders for the location and time of my husband's next assignment had changed no fewer than four times. First, we were leaving in March to one state. Then another in April. Finally, we have written orders sending us to my hometown of Tampa, Fla. for three years. I am 20 weeks pregnant with our fourth baby; we are six weeks away from a Virginia to Florida move and we don't have a home or an official move date yet. Frustrating? Sometimes. But the uncertainty that comes with our military lifestyle has cultivated resilience and flexibility in our family.

Three days ago we found out my husband, Mike, was able to travel to Florida for a week for house hunting leave. We are grateful for military travel options that helped us avoid spending $2,000+ on last-minute round trip tickets for the five of us.

We rouse our 5-, 3- and 1-year-olds from their beds. They slept in their travel clothes so are already dressed. My middle child is especially excited to go to "Por-ida to swim at the waterpark." We have a small meltdown because the shorts he is wearing are not his "bay-bing suit." I pull the individual servings of soaked oats I prepared from the fridge and we groggily load the little ones into the car. We are running just a few minutes behind schedule.

At the terminal, Mike goes inside to check in while I

37

unload our luggage onto a cart. Three car seats, one large suitcase (a miracle), a small carry-on, our breakfast, loveys, kids' activity backpacks…They fit on the cart, albeit in a heaping pile.

Check-in is smoother than when flying commercially and we board the plane. My daughter, the youngest, sobs and resists her carseat with every ounce of her strength. Other passengers look at the commotion, most with sympathetic smiles. I am grateful the flight is not full, and that my husband is actually travelling with us (for a change).

6:30. We have been awake for three hours and are headed to Florida. The kids eat breakfast. The baby wails a little more and settles eventually. I watch the sun rise from above the clouds. I soak in the serenity of the moment.

When we arrive, we pick up a minivan rental. The upside: We were first in line and avoided what could have been an hour-plus wait at the terminal. The downside: the car is filthy. I grab the open cup of coffee still in the cupholder just before my three-year-old takes a swig and spills it. Mike pulls a half-full bottle of gin from under the passenger seat. We are relieved we found it first and really can't do anything but
make a joke.

We have a three-hour drive ahead of us. The kids are cranky. Two start to cry. The novelty of the toys and videos and car entertainment fade. Eventually we stop for lunch. They stretch their legs and we begin again. We try to keep the mood light as the thunderstorm begins.

Once we arrive, we will be viewing homes that we have seen online and that some of my family members have graciously toured for us. Our goal is to determine the area we will live in, find a home to purchase, place a contract and begin the closing process within the next seven days. I can't begin to express how grateful I am that we have family in the area that can help with childcare during this week.

Years ago I would have thought this entire scenario was completely absurd. Today, it is par for the course. The babies are finally sleeping. I put on my headphones and close my eyes. We are almost here.

http://thecreativemama.com/military-move/

This chapter may seem rather negative, but I wanted to provide some insight into why this period is such a difficult one. While each relocation brings with it its own challenges, it is important to recognize that moves have positive aspects as well. With each move we meet new people, see new places, and experience new things. Without the military I wouldn't have met my husband or many of my dear and close friends. Moving is hard, and it always involves a lot of work and a lot of stress; but it has also helped me grow, mature, and develop into the person I am today.

MAIN MISCONCEPTIONS REGARDING MOVING

WRONG: Moving becomes easier over time.
TRUE: Contrary to most people's beliefs, moving does not get easier over time. And the fact that every family within the military has to go through similar changes does not soften the impact on each individual family either. What may get easier for some military families is the organizational part of a move itself, but the actual mental process within each one of us does not.

WRONG: The packing and moving is quite easy, as others do it for us.
TRUE: While we can choose to have a professional moving company pack up and move all our belongings, it is still an exhausting process, as the hardest part of moving is the stress associated with the preparations. Actual moving takes only 2-3 days, but it takes weeks to clear the installation, cancel all the bills, close out work projects, prepare the house, prepare the cars, get childcare or school set up, and find a new place to live.

WRONG: We can leave the military like we could any other job.
TRUE: Being in the military is associated with a certain service commitment, a period of obligated military service. Everyone who joins the military for the first time incurs a minimum eight-year service commitment.

WRONG: Making friends comes easy to us and takes no time, whatsoever.
TRUE: While most of us have more or less become accustomed to having to make new friends fast, the fact is that the establishment of a friendship has to be organic on some level and takes time, just like any other relationship.

5

OUR CULTURE
- For Tara -

*"...America's Soldiers, Sailors,
Marines, Airmen, and Coast
Guardsmen serve day and night
around the globe to defend our
Nation. We are all very proud of
them, and yet we should never
forget that none of them do it
alone. The extraordinary families
who support them sacrifice every
bit as much to make their service
possible... Our combat readiness
stems from readiness at home, and
America's might is a reflection of
the power of military families."*

Admiral Mike Mullen,
Chairman of the Joint Chiefs of Staff

Some people believe that being in the military is no different than working for a major corporation with multiple outlets around the world. But what corporation do you know that inspires the degree of loyalty and commitment that military service does?

By having joined the military, we have become part of a tightly knit community of people supporting a cause greater than ourselves. In this chapter, I would like to help you understand the military culture by defining what drives, motivates, and connects us.

In its simplest terms, a culture can be described as the customary beliefs and behaviors of a social group. So what are those particular beliefs and behaviors that evidently differ so much from yours that they caused your service(wo)man to emerge within a different cultural group?

Ask 100 people why they chose to *join* the military and you'll probably get about 100 different answers. They might include patriotism, travel, thrills, opportunities, money, and benefits. Many choose service as a way of upholding family tradition. Others grew up as military brats and might be unable to imagine any other life, as this is all they know. Yet others are looking for job security or opportunities to learn new skills and better themselves. The benefits of the GI Bill still draw people looking for a way to finance a college education. But though there are definite financial benefits to military service, not too many people are going to say that they did it solely for the money. So what keeps people in, despite deployments, family separations, and constant moves? Simply said, it's the belief in something bigger than oneself. Ask 100 people why they chose to *stay* in the military and you'll probably only get a handful of answers that include honor, pride, and a desire to serve their country.[11]

The military seems to draw together a diverse group of people from all walks of life. However, that mutual bond of believing in something bigger than oneself ensures a commonality that creates one single baseline amongst this diverse group of people.

It almost seems like we have built our own little community around ourselves. But how and why did this come about? Civilian friendships are formed over shared experiences such as attending the same schools, playing in the same team, or living in the same town for an entire life; all in a more or less stationary sense. But because we don't have this option of staying someplace for very long, we have to construct our own "stationary world on wheels." What this means is that we all have to relocate frequently, but we do so in the same circles under similar circumstances.

Even though we must move from base to base, it is not uncommon that one of our military friends has also lived in that very same town (although at different times), and attended the same base schools. This, in turn, creates a certain sense of commonality and camaraderie. Thriving networks of informal communications exist throughout military communities. We understand one another because we live through similar circumstances. We can relate to what the other one is going through because we have walked in those shoes. Military friends become an extended family; family that we can count on throughout and beyond our time in the service. Within our world, it does not matter how long or how short of a period we have actually known each other. We simply know that we are there for and can count on each other.

We are no longer in charge of our lives. Of course, we still have some input, but ultimately, our lives are out of our hands. This is a notion that can be hard to accept; but acceptance is necessary in order to find some sort of peace within the military. It's all about the perspective one chooses to adopt. While there are many things we can't control, there are just as many opportunities that the military lifestyle has presented to us that otherwise would have been impossible for us to attain or pursue. What we had to learn to come to terms with was simply to focus on the things that we can control and let go of those that we can't.

The existence of a cultural gap between the military and civilian world is only natural. People in the two cultures live drastically different lives and, increasingly, have different values. But today's military is an "all-volunteer force," which implies that no one is here who didn't choose to embrace the military values.[12]

But who are the actual members within this military society? The following is divided into three sections, in which I will discuss your service(wo)man him or herself, the spouse of your service(wo)man, and of course, the children of your service(wo)man.

SERVICE(WO)MAN

The military branches, and the many different jobs within each branch, are so diverse that it would be impossible to make any generalizations about the work day of any one military member.

Whichever of the five branches of the United States Armed forces — Army, Air Force, Navy, Marines, or Coast Guard — being part of this extensive team means more than just a high and tight haircut and target practice. Members of the military are leaders, organizers, strategists, and managers whose duties entail enormous responsibilities.[13]

Each branch of the armed forces has a particular function. The Army is the main ground-force of the United States. The Air Force defends through exploitation of air and space. The Navy's primary mission is to maintain the freedom of the seas. The Marine Corps provides the Navy with land support. And the Coast Guard is primarily concerned with law enforcement and illegal immigration control during peacetime, while in times of conflict, it can be transferred to the Department of the Navy.

All different, yet all the same: young men and women of the U.S. Military, doing their jobs each and every day. They are prepared to go to work here, or abroad, ready to make sacrifices to keep this nation safe and great!

Military practices are thorough, disciplined, and demanding. Working conditions vary greatly, but in all cases, standards of appearance and behavior are regulated. While forty-hour weeks are common, many must work odd, long hours. The perks, on the other hand, include extensive travel and health-care benefits, as well as family-oriented services like day care, job security, and a decent pension after a relatively short career.

So, what is a typical day in the military like? Let me start by boldly stating that the military seems to do more before 9am than most people do all day. The military is not a typical 9-5 job. Your service(wo)man is expected to be ready for duty 24/7. Yes, there are some days when your service(wo)man gets to go home early, but then there are other days when he or she doesn't get to go home at all.

What a day looks like depends on many things, for example whether the service member is on deployment or is getting ready for deployment. A regular work day counts an average of 7-9 hours, from Monday through Friday. If your service(wo)man is deployed, however, he or she is "on duty" all the time for the entire duration of the deployment, standing daily watches and not getting weekends off for months at a time.

The main thing I want you to understand is that a job within the military is not comparable to a regular civilian job. A contracted set of hours and a regulation of overtime do not exist. If the military needs the service member to work 24 hours a day, he or she will be working 24 hours a day. In practice, this will rarely be the case, but the point is that a service member is practically owned by the military, 365 days a year, 24 hours a day. It can be exhausting and challenging, but that is what is required of them.

Despite these demands, however, most service members love what they do. In fact, many people who leave the military before retirement find themselves filled with regret and often return to the service later. This, in turn, indicates that despite the long hours and hard work, many remain fiercely dedicated to their chosen career.

MILITARY SPOUSE
- For Erin -

On our wedding day, most of us didn't realize that, in addition to marrying our military spouse, we married into the lifestyle and culture of the military. We didn't just become a spouse, but a military spouse, and as the saying goes, "It's the toughest job in the military." This is true, no matter what branch.

Now, what does the life of a military spouse look like? Every military spouse has a story to tell. Those stories can be humorous or heartbreaking, but no two are alike. Military spouses' lives are just as diverse as those of our service(wo)men described above. Therefore, I would like to share this wonderful post of which the author, Judy Davis, has graciously given me permission to reprint. It so perfectly sums up our feelings, thoughts, and opinions regarding our military community without leaving any room for generalization.

Army Life: Dysfunctional, Unpredictable, Crazy, Fun and Worthwhile!

By Judy Davis – The Direction Diva
http://thedirectiondiva.com

Never take the line at Starbucks for granted! Ahhh…the line at Starbucks early on a Sunday Morning. It's almost as delicious as my Venti Non-Fat No Water Chai [btw....if you haven't had one...you gotta try it ...tell them Judy sent you ;)] …….but anyway back to my story.

The lady 2 people ahead of me obviously straight from the gym, toned arms and all (I think I hate her); then there is the army wife with 3 kids in tow just trying to get some caffeine so she can re-start her already hectic day (been there done that); the group of guys who, if I had to bet on it, haven't been home since last night and are debating whether to pull an all-dayer to go with their all-nighter (so glad my college days are behind me); the soldier who obviously got stuck with duty this weekend trying to stay awake for a few more hours 'til his relief gets in….And then there is me – straight from the muddy dog park, after dropping my husband off early for yet another week away in the field – my hair in a ponytail, no makeup, covered in paw prints and smelling like the gourmet salmon flavored dog treats that are extra smelly just so my puppy pays attention when every other scent is tickling her nostrils (btw… it doesn't work).

But here we are, all of us and our different lives in line waiting together and instantly we bond over what is the common thread – our "ArmyStrong-ness." Small conversations start up because we are all here waiting for the doors to open and we have to pass the time somehow (oh, did I forget to mention that I wasn't the only one who thought it opened earlier than it does on Sunday?).

Beautiful arm lady is anxiously waiting for her husband to return from a long year in Afghanistan; she can't wait to see him and tell him in person that she reached her goal of losing 75 pounds while he was gone. My group of "party boys" all "newbies" to the Army leave for the same place within the week and are admittedly a bit frightened. The mom with the kids…her husband left this morning to go back to the sandbox after a much needed 2 weeks of R&R and she's really not sure how she's gonna get through the day. And well the rest of us have the usual "Army life stuff" going on and are just doing our best to find the bright spot in every day.

But the amazing part is that in this line there is no rank, there is no judgment, there is no "my situation is worse than yours," and there is no "feel sorry for me." It's just a group of people who "get" what each other's lives are like, and in the sharing of our experiences we end up supporting each other without even trying. Maybe it's the fact that it's so beautiful out, or because it's early on a Sunday it could even be that we all feel a little raw today, but it's moments like this that make me proud to be in the "military family."

Nowhere else can such a diverse group of people come together and form instant bonds. Nowhere else would frightened soldiers help out a frantic mom by holding her baby while she ran for her toddler. Nowhere else would a muddy, hair pulled up, paw printed, dog-treat-smelling spouse who hadn't had caffeine yet, feel so welcome. Nowhere else but in this line, on this post and in this "family." And the funny thing is that this family changes daily, new faces, new outfits, new situations… But at the root of it, we all have a silent bond that is ours to share no matter where we are, what line we are in, or who we are standing next to.

> Yep, it's times like this that I'm proud to be part of this dysfunctional, crazy, fun and unpredictable group of people that have become MY military family.
>
> http://dailydirectionmoments.wordpress.com/2012/04/01/my-dysfunctional-intense-crazy-fun-and-unpredictable-military-family/

Such a diverse group of people, yet so many things they have in common. Forget having to keep up with the Joneses in its most traditional sense. The military creates a common ground, thereby acting as some sort of equalizer. When everyone wears uniforms, shops at the same stores, belongs to the same clubs, sends their kids to the same schools, and shows up at the same hospitals, getting ahead does not seem to be a concern anymore.

Some spouses truly enjoy military life. Others do not and struggle with it almost on a daily basis. But no matter how we feel about life in the military, it takes a great deal of dedication and sacrifice on our part.

No one is more proficient and adept in keeping education and employment flexible than a military spouse! Seriously, think about it! How long did it take you to complete your education? How long did it take to get the job you've wanted for so long? How long does it usually take to climb that corporate ladder? While most people dedicate the majority of their adult lives to these pursuits, military spouses don't have the luxury of sticking around to finish their degree or work on their career and build seniority. Transferring credits from one university to another greatly impacts a spouse's ability to finish a degree or continue moving up in a chosen career path.

Many spouses started their degree at one institution only to graduate a couple of different universities later. And what military spouse doesn't have numerous gaps in his or her resume with an eccentric and seemingly unrelated collection of jobs held over the years? My resume is a perfect example of such patchwork-like occupational experiences. An in Germany registered nurse, that after having moved to the U.S. studied International Affairs, then taught English and German, received her MA in Accounting and Financial Management, and went back to teaching again (Accounting & Finance this time). It can be quite challenging to balance the necessary moves in support of the service member and the spouse's own desire to create a life and career for him or herself.

High cost of out-of-state college tuition, expenses associated with having to pay for certification and licensure every time one moves across state lines, and lag time for spouses to find jobs when they move are only a few of the issues military spouses have to face after relocation.

Finding a new job can be stressful for anyone, but it can be especially challenging for military spouses, as we must go through the process often due to our frequent moves. Frequent relocation can be disruptive to a career, particularly in view of the fact that many employers (especially in civilian communities) are often quite hesitant to hire a person associated with the military for fear that this person will only be working there for a short period of time.

We often have to take a job that is below our skill level just so that we have a job. I know of military spouses that are licensed attorneys working in the tax assistance center, certified public accountants working as bank tellers, MBA holders working in payroll, and nurses working as tutors. But that is okay. We've long come to realize that the most important attribute to aspire toward within this lifestyle is flexibility. We may not get to work in the same industries as at our last jobs, but we may still be able to use many of the same skills while gaining valuable new ones for the future. No one is more accommodating and adjusting than military spouses when it comes to education and employment. So remember, if you have the chance to hire a military spouse, jump at the opportunity because you won't find many people that are as capable, compassionate, or adaptable.

I asked some of my friends to complete this sentence "You know you're a military spouse when…" Here are some of their answers:

YOU KNOW YOU'RE A MILITARY SPOUSE WHEN…

- …You get to see your spouse about 2 months out of the year.
- …You make a great friend, but have to say goodbye again because one of you has to move halfway around the country or world.
- …Your amazon account has at least five shipping addresses.
- …You find yourself sacrificing just as much for your country as your spouse.
- …You find it unusual (but wonderful) having your spouse home on your birthday or any other major holiday.
- …You're searching for change (USD) and all you can find is Euros.
- …After a move, you tell yourself that unpacking is just not worth it.
- …You have more friends in places around the world than you do in your current location.
- …You have children born in 3 different states or even countries.
- …After being in one location for 3 or 4 years, you start thinking it is time to move again.
- …A marriage anniversary is celebrated via Skype, as your spouse is in a warzone thousands of miles away.
- …You stop calling your hometown "home" and start realizing "home" is where your spouse is, no matter the place.
- …You know the exact weight and value of your entire household goods.
- …While your spouse is deployed, you make friends for life with others around you who are going through the same things.
- …Even your three-year-old can use the acronym "PTSD" (Post-Traumatic Stress Syndrome) in a sentence correctly.
- …None of your civilian friends really understands your life anymore.

MILITARY WIDOW(ER)
- For Katie -

"We regret to inform you..." Hearing these terrifying words is every military spouse's worst nightmare. The military is made up of hundreds of thousands of men and women of character and integrity. Each has volunteered to protect and defend America and, if need be, make the ultimate sacrifice in its defense. Truthfully, however, every military service member expects to leave this earth via a more or less natural departure. Sometimes, though, life doesn't turn out the way it's planned.[14]

Since 2001, according to the U.S. Department of Defense, over 6,500 U.S. service members have been killed in Iraq and Afghanistan. Around half of these service members were married, leaving an estimated 3,200 military widows across our country from these wars alone. These numbers do not include our heroes who lost their lives in non-combat activities, leaving countless more military widows. While the service member's sacrifice is acknowledged, many simply forget or fail to recognize the sacrifice of the spouse who is now left a military widow. Oftentimes, the invisible wounds of military widows are disregarded due to age or a simple lack of knowledge and understanding.[15]

The widow(er) left behind lost much more than a heroic service member; the loss is life changing. From this point forward, time will be measured by the years spent with the service(wo)man and the years spent without him or her.

Military widow(er)s come in all ages, races, nationalities, and religions, with spouses of all rates, ranks, and service branches. All military widow(er)s walk the same path, one filled with unknown and sometimes scary obstacles, as they work to survive their loss and cope with the feelings, thoughts, and issues that confront them.[16]

In most western cultures, we usually think of a

widow(er) as an older person, such as our grandfathers or grandmothers. But in reality, most military widow(er)s are in their twenties, thirties, or forties. Because military widow(er)s aren't supposed to be a widow(er) at such a young age, they can feel like they don't fit in anywhere. The world tells them that they are not married, but they don't feel single. They probably wonder where they belong, and might feel alone and isolated at times.

One of the best books on military widows is *"Military Widow: A Survival Guide"* by Joanne M. Steen. It was written for the military widow, but is also meant for the parent, in-law, relative or friend of one of America's fallen warriors. The book helps to understand military widowhood from the widow(er)'s perspective. Military grief is complex and often burdened with circumstances not normally found in the civilian world. A military death is most likely unexpected, potentially traumatic, possibly in another country, publicized by the media, and enveloped in the commitment to duty and country. In addition, military widow(er)s are young, often with young families, and are living at a duty station, far away from family and long-time friends.[17]

Sometimes, especially in situations in which people don't know what to say, we bluntly start babbling without thinking. Those moments can produce the most hurtful remarks a widow(er) ever hears. There is little we can say to make it better, but a lot we can say to make it worse...

What follows is only a small sample of thoughtless and inappropriate comments military widow(er)s have to listen to simply because people do not understand the depth of their loss and grief.

- When you married into the military you should have been prepared for your husband to die.
- It was a good thing he died first because he wouldn't have wanted to live without you...
- I know it's hard to believe it now, but someday you'll meet somebody new.
- Well, you'll be fine. You're a strong person. You'll go on with your life.
- Do you have a boyfriend yet?
- Wow, you've lost a lot of weight! What diet are you on?
- You're young; you have your whole life ahead of you.
- Give it a year, you'll see. You'll find someone else.
- It's harder for you because you don't have children.
- Are you done crying yet?
- Wow, you don't look like a widow!
- It's part of God's plan.
- I know just how you feel - I had to put my dog down last year.
- You'll probably come to enjoy being your own boss again.

http://www.dailystrength.org

Those kinds of misguided remarks are common during a widow(er)'s grief. While some of these statements might have been extended with good intentions, they are remarkably insensitive!

What can you do to help a widow(er)? What should you say? Here are a few suggestions about what you could say to a newly widowed person.

- Please do stay connected. There is already a huge hole in a widow(er)'s universe. Do not assume they need 'space' to grieve.

- Acknowledge the situation. Please do say you are sorry for their loss. They'd rather you tell them you do not know what to say than tell them your story of losing your friend or even close relative.

- Do refer to our husband's and wives' acts or words—serious or humorous. Widow(er)s are so comforted by knowing their husbands and wives have not been forgotten. Do not leave them out of your conversations.

- Do call and ask specifically, "Can we go for a walk together? May run errands for you? Meet you for coffee?"

- Invite widow(er)s to anything. They may decline but will appreciate being asked.

http://www.widowconnection.com

I thought it important to include this part on military widow(er)s, as many (including myself) don't really know how to react and what to say when someone tells us that their significant other has passed away.

As this chapter is solely about us, the military family, I only included the side of the military widow(er) in an attempt to make you as the reader aware of their existence and their difficulties they have to face. I realize that parents have lost their children and friends have lost their companions, but this section was intentionally written about the spouses left behind, in order to increase understanding of and mitigate ignorance toward our military widow(er)s.

Sometimes, we don't bother to find out what these widow(er)s have to go through because we don't really want to know and choose to be and remain ignorant. While they struggle with their grief, it seems that those around them find it easier to simply move on with their lives. Why is that? I believe many of us avoid military widow(er)s as they represent our deepest fears; the unspoken fear that our service(wo)man could be next.

We don't want to know how much they are aching

each and every day. We don't want to know how painful it is to know that their service(wo)man will never be able to return to them. It is all too intimidating and horrible for us. Too uncomfortable. Too real. We want them to forget as fast as possible so that we can move on with our lives without this dreadful lurking fear that something could happen to our very own service(wo)man. All that I realized after I met my very first military widow. I can't believe how ignorant I had been before I heard her story. So many had chosen to distance themselves from her after her husband passed away. So many had judged her without ever haven taken the opportunity of getting to know her and her story. You may have been estranged from your loved one in the military, but when they become a widow(er), they need you more than ever as they may have no one else. I came to realize that the toughest job in the military is not being a military wife. The toughest job is being a military widow(er).

FOREIGN-BORN MILITARY SPOUSES
- For Patricia -

Imagine yourself in a place where everybody speaks another language that you barely understand. No one but you speaks your mother tongue; no one but you understands your cultural values. You are hundreds of thousands of miles away from home, your family and your friends. You are, in a sense, completely alone. This is what most foreign-born spouses feel like when they first move to the United States.

What follows is an experience shared by a young woman, and expresses and mirrors my thoughts and my own experiences as a 20-year-old German coming to this country many years ago.

"A friend of mine met a very sweet young German woman at her son's school on Friday. She arrived in the U.S. two weeks ago, and oh boy, when I heard this it brought back some memories. Right about now she is at that stage where she is thinking: "What the hell did I do?" She gave up her family, her friends, her independence, her job, her apartment, her language, her way of life, her traditions, her culture. She gave up... her LIFE as she knew it. And she did it for LOVE. Not because she wanted to be in America, or because everything is better here, or because she always dreamed of seeing the WORLD. Nope, she gave it up for love, plain and simple. So please, the next time you meet a foreigner and you get frustrated because his or her English is not up to par, or because she acts differently than you are used to, be KIND anyway. It's not easy to give up everything you've known and loved. I have been asked how much I paid my husband for bringing me here and I said "I gave him my life."

The life of the military spouse brings with it a unique set of challenges and responsibilities, as previously discussed. Add that a number of military spouses are not born and raised in America, and we have a whole new set of issues to cope with when moving to America, both as an immigrant AND as a new military spouse, as this essentially means having to adapt to two new cultures at the same time: the military culture and the American culture.[18] While this situation brings many opportunities, it is also filled with challenges.

A very important part of a person's make-up, apart from their native language, are other aspects of their culture that set them apart as unique, such as their food, music, view of the world and traditions. Many foreign-born military spouses will want to hold tight to those aspects, not wanting to compromise or drop what they hold dear and have known for so long. So while Americans call it their tradition to open Christmas presents on Christmas Day on December 25th, for example, many Europeans tend to open gifts on the 24th, on Christmas Eve. Other examples might include traditions regarding birthdays, meal preparations, and acceptable social norms and behaviors.

As implied by the recited experience above, many foreign-born spouses have to fight the stigma and assumptions of having married a service member in order to be able to live in this country. This thought, however, is incredibly prejudiced and arrogant, as it implies that the foreign-born spouse's homeland is secondary and inferior to that of the U.S. It also indirectly questions a couple's relationship and primary reason for getting married: love. Unfortunately, this train of thought is common, especially among those who have never been abroad and have never been truly exposed to other cultures.

Many foreign-born military spouses feel isolated and alone when first moving to the U.S., as communication can be difficult. They have no easy access to their first language, apart from the times they speak to their family and friends back home. Adjusting to a new culture can be a time of confusion, stress, and anxiety, which amounts to the phenomenon known as "culture shock".

The symptoms of culture shock usually differ from person to person, and may include feeling lonely or mildly depressed, stressed or irritable, and wanting to isolate from others.[19] Foreign-born spouses may feel overwhelmed trying to absorb all of the new aspects of living in the United States. At times, they may feel homesick. They may even feel hesitant and insecure about themselves as they try to figure out how to properly behave according to local customs.

A principal element of conflict arises when children become part of the equation, as involved parties may disagree about how they ought to be brought up. Raising children in a multi-cultural setting can be quite challenging. Let's take language as an example. Nowadays, many parents try to expose their children to a second language other than English in order to prepare them academically. For other families like mine, raising multilingual children is just one way to ensure that our kids are accepting and aware of their diverse cultural heritage. I fiercely compete with English taught at school and everywhere else outside our home. It is my duty to keep my native language alive in our home for the sake of preserving my cultural heritage in my children.

In a multicultural marriage, you are not just uniting two individuals; you are bringing together two different worldviews. If, therefore, your service(wo)man is married to a foreign-born spouse, be aware of all these possible differences, and try to find ways to incorporate the different cultural aspects into your family or circle of friendship. Try to have a positive attitude and respect for the spouse's culture and traditions.

Cultural clashes and misunderstandings are generally inevitable if you do not take the time to educate yourself about the culture, background, and other aspects of upbringing of your service(wo)man's foreign-born spouse. In the Chinese culture, for example, asking a stranger questions is a normal way to show sympathy and to invite someone to have a friendly conversation. Western culture, on the other hand, is based on individualism, and might therefore consider it impolite to insist on communication through questions.

It's easy to judge quickly without trying to get to know a person, but try not to, no matter what place a foreign-born spouse calls his or her home. Don't look down on them or make assumptions of their reasons for being here, but rather, welcome the different and unique experiences the foreign-born spouse may expose you to. After all, your service(wo)man loves this person, so you should too.

MILITARY KIDS

> Short essay on
> "My Life As A Military Child"
> By Amber
> 3rd Grade
>
> My life is different, yours may not be.
> I see things kids should not have to see.
> Living so far away, I still see him in the front of my mind.
> I know he's away protecting mankind.
> The days feel so lonely without him,
> And sadness fills my heart to the rim.
> Really needing his strong embrace,
> Yet I'm not even able to see his face.
>
> Crying at night until my eyes are nearly drowned,
> Hoping like crazy he comes home safe and sound.
> It takes massive strength to be a military kid,
> Living life each day trying not to flip my lid.
> Dad, I love you and I miss you when you are gone.
>
> http://www.funatwarren.com/wp-content/uploads/2009/11/Essay-Booklet-for-Web2.pdf

Your service(wo)man willingly chose the military as a way of life by signing up for the service. And military spouses, for the most part, knew what they were getting into when they married a service member. The third member of our military family, the military child, however, had no such choice.

"Military brats," a term of endearment and respect within military culture, have the same needs as any other children. They too crave structure and routine, which in turn provides them with a sense of reassurance and security. They too want to see and get spoiled by their grandparents. They too want to experience unconditional love and support from family and friends.

As previously discussed, military life is marked by

frequent relocations and often means having to live far away from extended family. The National Military Family Association estimates that the average military child moves 6 to 9 times between kindergarten and high school.[20] Imagine how potentially difficult this is for kids who may not always understand why they have to say goodbye to their friends yet again. It never gets easier to leave your friends behind, no matter how often you have to move.

It is hard enough making friends in school. Factor in a move every two to three years and you might begin to understand the challenges our military kids have to face. Regardless of their type of schooling, military children may have a difficult time maintaining continuity throughout their school experience, as each state has different graduation requirements. Our children's anxiety of having to start all over again is compounded by their fear of being behind because they're possibly starting a new school months after the official first day, as moving times don't always coincide with the beginning and end of a school year.[20] These are just some of the many challenges military children have to face that most simply don't ever think or worry about.

But who would be better equipped and able to describe their own lives than the military kids themselves?

Sarah 10th Grade	Kayla 7th Grade
My life as a military child always consisted of adapting to my habitat no matter where my family was stationed. One thing the military taught me was to seize the day. Moving from place to place every three years, people come and go, meaning you need to appreciate the days with the people that you have while you have them. While living in Germany, seizing the day was easy. But, seeing my friend's parents deploy and knowing my parents could also deploy any minute made me appreciate my family a lot more. My parents taught me respect and molded my morals from the lives they lived in the military. Just because I am a teenager doesn't mean that the military didn't enter my heart too. Without the military, I would never be the same because though I am a part of the military, the military is part of me too.	Life in the military has had a great impact in my life with good and bad memories associated in the process of my dad's achievements. Many times my dad has had to leave me and my mom by ourselves for months or even years. Although it was the hardest thing to say goodbye, it has helped me to become a stronger person on the inside and learn to sacrifice by having the ones that I love leave and not knowing if they will return. Also, life in the military has impacted me by helping me learn how I need to cherish the time that I have with my loved ones. Life is precious and can be here one minute but can be taken away from us the next minute. I'm glad to be part of the military family which has helped me learn many valuable life lessons.

I personally find it quite interesting that 7th graders already concern themselves with the notion of "seizing the moment" and "cherishing the time with loved ones," something I didn't learn to appreciate or even seriously consider until adulthood. Our way of life, then, is arguably the principal factor that shapes and influences the social development of our offspring within this community.

Studies show that this group is very much shaped by frequent moves, both in a positive and negative way. Military children become quite adaptive, as they have to experience a constant loss of friendships. This, in turn, causes them to facilitate an ability to make new friends more easily and quickly, but may also hinder a concrete development of emotional attachments to people and places, due to this transitory lifestyle. A constantly changing environment has its benefits, but also comes with a price. Rather than develop problem-solving skills, there is a temptation to simply leave a problem without resolving it, as the next move is not too far away.

For most of their lives, military children will not have an actual hometown, but instead, will experience an extensive exposure to a wide range of regional as well as foreign cultures and languages. They often grow and develop in the absence of a parent due to deployments, which in turn exposes them to extraordinary stresses of knowing a loved one is working in a combat zone.

In homes where both parents are serving, there will be times during which a family will have to face long periods of geographical separation. Unless the two service member parents can always get assigned to the same installation, chances are that, in addition to the occasional deployments, they may also be given different assignment locations.

Raising happy, well-adjusted children in the military can be quite demanding. And doing so without the immediate help and support of one's extended family makes this task all the more challenging. Being a grandparent is a wonderful thing, and many have had to wait a long time to be blessed with grandchildren. The reality surrounding military families is, however, that once those long longed for grandchildren finally do enter your lives, they are usually not able to remain close to you geographically, as they are destined to tag along to your service(wo)man's next assignment. As it can be very hard to be away from one's grandchildren, the result is quite often the development of a certain degree of resentment towards your service(wo)man's lifestyle. While this emotion is quite understandable, please know that it is just as hard (if not harder) on your service(wo)man and spouse to see their children having to grow up without their beloved grandparents.

The military institution is quite comparable to a family business that constitutes and maintains its very own and unique community. Is one member of the nuclear family part of it, so are all other members. It's everyone, or no one. It's all, or nothing. As the military spouse, one's own career necessitates flexibility in order to be able to conform to the serving member's professional obligations. And as the military child, one's character needs to be adaptable and accepting enough to be able to conform to new and ever-changing situations.

Across all the branches of the military, be it the Air Force, Army, Marine Corps, Navy, or Coast Guard, common ideals and values are taught reinforced; ideals such as loyalty, integrity, and honor; as well as the development of character traits such as patriotism and adaptability. Oftentimes, military kids' sacrifices are taken for granted and don't quite receive the recognition they deserve. April is the month of the military child. Our military kids don't have an entire month dedicated to them by accident. It's an acknowledgement that they serve their country too.[21]

MILITARY COMMUNITY AS A WHOLE

So far, we've talked about the actual serving member of the military family, the spouses, and the kids. Those components combined in its plurality, then, make up our military community. As with most human communities, intent, belief, resources, preferences, needs, risks, and a number of other conditions are present and common amongst us, thereby affecting our identity and our degree of cohesiveness.[22]

The military unquestionably creates and retains its very own culture and community. Our culture is rich and steeped in tradition, history, and customs, while our community is involved in the present connectivity of our military families. The tightly knit members of our community support each other and a cause greater than ourselves.

It is somewhat frightening to think about having to move every two to three years into a completely new location with its very own distinguishing circumstances, and having to start all over again. Fortunately, the military provides us with a structured network that ensures that we have people, resources, and programs to support us.

Part of this support system is the option to live within a military installation. Choosing this option provides many with a fair amount of comfort, not only because it's a guarded community, but also because it signifies living among peers that experience similar circumstances and situations. While people living within a more traditional neighborhood come from all walks of life and represent a very broad spectrum of different careers and jobs, people living on a military installation have a similar background and the same employer.

People choose to live within a military installation for multiple reasons, a shared commonality being only one of them. At times, we find it quite comforting to know that others around us share similar experiences, especially during times of deployment. Knowing someone close that truly understands is an important benefit and of great value. Some, however, choose not to live on a military installation in order to better separate their private lives from work.

Military service is a demanding way of life and there are very few people willing to sign up for it, as evidenced by the one percent of our nation's population who make up this country's all-volunteer force. Our way of life is in a constant state of uncertainty, something that can be quite difficult for civilians to comprehend. Very often we get asked what to expect in the next couple of years to come, when we are planning to move again, where we're intending to move, and for how long we anticipate to remain. If we were part of the civilian world, those types of questions wouldn't be hard to answer. But in the context of our military lives, others know as much about our future as we do. We don't have the answers. And if we do try to answer those questions too prematurely, our circumstances are just going to change again anyway. Nothing is written in stone. Nothing is for certain. Our lives are constantly changing, and we have no choice but to simply accept it and adjust accordingly. We don't really have the luxury to plan; we react.

Could I describe my military life in just six words? I would have to get right to the point and decide what's most important to me. This exercise was featured on usaa.com. The first time this exercise was used was reportedly in the 1920s. Ernest Hemmingway was challenged to write an entire short story using only six words. His evocative story was this: "For sale. Baby shoes. Never worn."

Here are a couple of examples of how the military life has been described using only six words:

> I was blessed. I still am.
> Honor, Pride, Integrity, Service, Devotion, Family.
> I would fight for your freedoms.
> Born – Enlisted – Deployed – Insured – Survived – Retired.
> Once A Marine. Always A Marine.
> A Life Worth Living.
> One Family, United, under God, forever.
> Saved by grace…Called to serve.
> My god, my family, my country.
> Live to Serve…Serve to Live.
> …Because it's an Honor to Serve.
> Annual Mission Trip: Giving To Others.
> Amazing Grace How Sweet The Sound.
> Greatest sacrifices: Time with loved ones.
> Once a Soldier, Today… Tomorrow… Forever.
>
> https://www.usaa.com/inet/pages/lh_lifeins_6wordslp_landing_mkt?adid=VURL_6words

This chapter was not meant to compare civilian and military societies with one another. A society needs values from both ends of a spectrum: kindness and discipline, toughness and sensitivity. Those values, while counterparts at the surface, should reinforce instead of weaken one another. In a democracy with a large standing military, mutual understanding is essential.

While military families have the same life experiences common to many families, including balancing work and family, parenting issues, and maintaining healthy relationships, they also have unique stressors relating to the requirements of their service member's employment. Many factors of military family life, including frequent separation and the subsequent reintegration process and increased frequency of relocation, produce stressors that need to be addressed in order to maintain satisfaction within both the military and family environments.[23] In an attempt to address and mitigate one of those main stressors, the following chapter will concern itself with and discuss the issues of deployment. By educating and informing you about this very real and very life-disrupting subject matter, I hope to lessen the emotional and mental load a military family will have to carry during those difficult times by inspiring you to support and encourage us during those challenging periods via your understanding, sympathy, empathy, and actions.

MAIN MISCONCEPTIONS REGARDING MILITARY CULTURE

WRONG: A military job is the same as a civilian job.
TRUE: A job within the military is not comparable to a regular civilian job. A contracted set of hours and a regulation of overtime do not exist. A service member is practically owned by the military, 365 days a year, 24 hours a day.

WRONG: Most military spouses prefer to stay home.
TRUE: We've heard all the stereotypes before: military spouses are fat, lazy, and live off of other taxpayers' hard-earned money. While many actually do earn their own paychecks, others are not that lucky to have a portable career. The fact of the matter is that maintaining a career is very challenging for military spouses, as they support their service members by moving with them.

WRONG: Foreign-born-spouses married a service member in order to receive a green card.
TRUE: The majority of foreign-born-spouses have not, as is often assumed, married a US citizen in order to come to America. They do not believe America to be better than their home country and love and miss it and relatives and friends in it. The majority of foreign-born-spouses in fact, married for love.

WRONG: We know what the next couple of years will bring.
TRUE: Our way of life is in a constant state of uncertainty. Very often we get asked what we expect for the years to come, when we are planning to move, where we're intending to go, and for how long we anticipate to remain there. The truth is that we don't even know where we'll be in 6 months. Our lives are constantly changing, and we have no choice but to adjust. We don't really have the luxury to plan; we react.

6

DEPLOYMENT
- For Amy -

Deployment is the military-related topic discussed most extensively within and outside of the military. While there aren't very many resources for the previously discussed topics specifically written for our nonmilitary family members and friends, resources on deployment are vast. As such, this chapter will not discuss how to prepare for deployment, or how to get through this period in one piece as you can find that extensively elsewhere; instead, it attempts to illustrate the subject of deployment from our perspectives in order to help you understand what we as the military family go through, experience, think, and feel during this trying time.

This chapter was one of the hardest for me to write, mainly because it caused me to relive some of the emotions I experienced during my husband's deployments. No matter if this is our first, third, or fifth time, deployment is an intense and unusual part of our lives.

It's an extremely important subject to us, mainly because it impacts our lives so completely. It's one of the largest sacrifices we as a military family can and have to make. Each family views and deals with deployments differently, but for me it is one of the most difficult times I face. As such, it is important for me to inform others, mainly our families and friends, about what a deployment truly means to us and our lives, and how you can help us through it.

I have been trying to avoid having to write about this topic, but it is a major part of our existence, and as such, a major distinction between us and any civilian family. Deployment is partially what defines us as a family unit, as it influences and impacts our lives so completely.

There is no one size fits all deployment; every deployment is different. The only commonality amongst most deployments is the fact that nothing is ever for certain, especially information regarding your service(wo)man's departure and return dates. This holds true mainly because scheduling depends on so many different factors such as aircraft availability and capacity, and unexpected changes in the dynamics of the mission.

The number and length of deployments also differ from service member to service member, depending on the deployee's branch of service, military specialty, unit, and mission. While some may deploy for year-long tours, others deploy for shorter periods, several times a year.

However, no matter the length, what always seems to hold true is the fact that those months go by faster for you than they do for us. 12 months – one entire year of our lives. A time during which we don't get to see each other, don't get to hold each other. Won't be able to fall asleep and wake up right next to each other. If there is ever a sacrifice that is being made by the military family, it's this missed time with each other.

To begin, I would like to define what "Deployment" actually means. According to the Department of Defense, military deployment is described as the movement of armed forces and their logistical support infrastructure around the world. Deployments consist of women and men leaving their families and their homes to go to another country in order to perform some type of mission.

Deployments may be for disaster relief, peace-keeping operations, or combat operations. These deployments can last anywhere from 90 days to 15 months, though the standard length for Army deployments has recently been reduced to 9 months. "Redeployment," then, designates the return of the service(wo)men to their prior duty station where their families live.

What does a deployment really mean to us? What does it really mean to you? What are the similarities and differences between the experiences and emotions we as a military family and you as a civilian encounter? Are those encounters comparable at all? In most cases, your service(wo)man, together with his/her family, is most likely stationed at a location far away from what you call your home. As such, time you get to spend together is likely to be limited to major occasions such as holiday visits. Consequently, you are more or less used to being apart from this part of your family or friends, at least geographically. What, then, is the difference between your service(wo)man being located at some regular domestically located military installation and a deployment location overseas? The difference is that one is located in a more controllable and known setting such as within the United States, whereas the other is most likely to be an international combat zone or part of a peace-keeping mission. While this, of course, is no minor difference and does indeed resemble a tremendously nerve-racking situation, it is one of the main characteristics that distinguishes your experience from ours as a military family. How so? We both undergo feelings such as fear, stress, and anticipation during the deployment, but on top of those emotions, the military family also experiences an abrupt separation from our service(wo)man. We experience an actual and real disruption to our daily lives.

This is not to say that you don't miss and don't worry about your service(wo)man. It is, however, meant to illustrate that, while our situations are somewhat similar, our experiences with a deployment as a military family unit are also very different from yours.

I have divided this chapter into five parts: 1) Getting the News, 2) The Deployment Process, 3) Common Misconceptions about Deployments, 4) Consequences of War, and 5) The Deployment from our Perspectives. Breaking down the chapter into these parts is meant to help you understand and see the deployment through our eyes, in order to gain understanding of how to support your service(wo)man and military family and keep personal communication strong throughout the duration of any deployment.

GETTING THE NEWS

LOOKING AT DIFFERENT PERSPECTIVES

The news of a pending deployment is perceived in many different ways, mainly depending on one's relationship to the person being deployed. Keeping this difference of perception in mind, I have tried to capture some of the thoughts and experiences each involved individual may go through.

SERVICE(WO)MAN

I have to leave again. How am I going to break the news to my family? What will my spouse say? How much will my child change within the year I am gone? Such life-changing events will take a while to sink in. I am experiencing a weird mixture of fear and excitement. After all, that's what I have been training for all this time. But should I wait to tell my parents? When is the best time to tell them? Will I have access to a phone or the internet and be able to contact my loved ones? How will my being away affect my relationship? Will my wife wait for me? I won't tell anyone until I am absolutely certain. Until then, it will be my emotional burden to carry. Here we go, another deployment that will put my own and my loved ones' lives on hold.

SPOUSE

I can't believe he has to leave again! I knew another deployment was coming, but I am in shock and completely overwhelmed by a number of feelings: fear, stress, loneliness, sadness, and maybe even a little resentment toward him for having to leave again. I'm dreading the next few days, weeks, and months to come. I'm dreading having to explain to my kids why Daddy isn't coming home at night. I'm dreading having to tell them that Daddy won't be able to come and read his bedtime story. I'm dreading this deployment. And while I truly want to support my service member, I can't help but wonder how I am going to get through each day of his deployment without being consumed by worries. This hurts. This is not what I planned for my life. A year is such a long time.

CHILD

I don't understand why Daddy has to leave again. Where is he going? Why can't he come home? Why did he want to go? I hate him being gone so much. I hate that he misses all my school recitals. Why can't he stay? Doesn't he want to see me in my next game? It's an important one! Why doesn't he understand that I need him here? I can't believe he is doing this to me again! Sometimes it feels like daddy is deployed more than he is home. I wish he would be home more. I will miss him so much! But I better not tell him. I don't want him to worry.

MILITARY PARENT

Why did she join the military? We knew this day, this deployment, had to come eventually, but we were secretly hoping that the subject would just somehow disappear. Of course we are proud of her, but we also feel a certain degree of fear and anxiety. I sure hate to see her go and leave her family behind. But they have the entire military community around them for support. We, on the other hand, have no one that knows and understands what we are going through. How should we behave now? Should we try to talk about it? We really would like to talk about our worries and fears, but would that hurt our daughter and her family? Should we just pretend we are okay with all of this? Should we just pretend and hold on to the belief that there is nothing to worry about?

CIVILIAN FRIEND

I can't believe he is about to deploy again. Didn't he just come back from a deployment? Well, they are military, so I'm sure they are already used to all of this. Time really does fly. And if I remember correctly, the last deployment went by fairly quickly. I do wonder how the family is holding up though. I should give them a call. Maybe there is something I can do to support them. I should definitely drop them a line to see how they are doing. Maybe tomorrow...

These are just some possibilities that describe how one can be confronted with deployment. For most, it is a very emotional time in which nothing really seems to be able to remedy the painful sentiments and feelings one is going through. While nothing can be done and nothing can be said that would truly make any of us feel better about the upcoming period of separation, do talk to us about it. Doing so will demonstrate to us that you, too, think about it and our loved one overseas. Ignoring an upcoming deployment out of fear of unintentionally hurting us, on the other hand, only causes us to think the opposite: that you simply chose to close your eyes to your own and our feelings. It's not always important what is being said. Sometimes, just seeing you try to understand us will satisfy our longing for care and compassion, which in turn makes us feel heard and loved. Communication, no matter to what degree, is very important, especially during times like these.

So here are some things you can and should say in order to support your military service(wo)man and his or her family:

- **"I don't know what you're going through, but I want to help. What do you need?"** - It's ok that you don't know how hard a deployment is. But you don't have to know what it's like to help. Just ask how you can help.
- **"Why don't you and the kids come have dinner with us tonight?"** - Invite us to BBQs, family dinners, ball games and other activities. Give us the chance to have a normal afternoon or evening with our family and friends. It's one of the best things you can do for us.
- **"I'd like to send a letter/card/package. What is the address?"**
- **"Call me anytime you need to talk."**
- **"Thank you"** – We don't do this for thanks, but even that small acknowledgment of the sacrifices that we make and the enormity of the struggles that we go through means the world to us.

THE DEPLOYMENT PROCESS

Deployments are an odd paradox. On the one hand, a deployment often represents the only opportunity a service(wo)man will have to actually perform the skills that he or she has trained on for months or years. On the other hand, everyone realizes that a deployment also means separation from friends, family, and the comforts associated with home.

While most service members spend their entire careers training for combat deployments, their families and friends usually do not. As such, family and friends are typically not trained to handle the emotional challenges that a deployment brings with it.

Being part of the military, every service member has to expect to be deployed and re-deployed. But as our country's operational commitments have increased throughout the world, military families are now often faced with deployments in even more rapid successions. It does not matter whether the mission is a combat operation, peace keeping, humanitarian or disaster relief; the outcome is the same: back to back deployments or trainings with varied lengths cause service(wo)men to spend more time away from their families.[24]

Deployment is a very emotional time for all involved. Below, you'll find an illustration which depicts the deployment cycle, followed by an expansion on each illustrated phase, including the actual deployment proceedings, as well as the emotional settings the deployed and his/her family will go through and experience during this time.

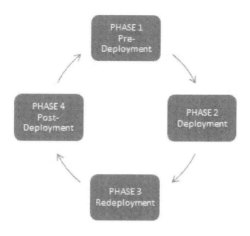

PHASE 1: PRE-DEPLOYMENT

The train-up and preparation stage focuses on the unit's and the service member's preparations for a military mission. Deployments rarely come as a surprise. Most deployments are planned months in advance, so units have sufficient time to prepare both mentally and physically. Train-up periods, including exercises and equipment preparation, are usually scheduled months before the actual deployment.

Most service(wo)men are excited by the prospect of their first deployment. Since they have no idea what to expect, they will assume that their experiences will resemble those depicted in movies or television shows. This initial excitement is quickly dampened by the incredible volume of work that must be done before a unit departs. Most units will conduct a substantial amount of individual level training as well as a mission rehearsal exercise of some type. In addition to this mandatory training, units must also spend a significant amount of time preparing and shipping various types of equipment. It's not uncommon for a unit to spend six months or more preparing for a deployment during which time the service member is working long hours almost daily. This is an exhausting time for everyone involved and it is made all the worse because the stress of the deployment continues to bear down like the sword of Damocles. In fact, most service members experience a degree of relief when the time comes to finally get on a plane and depart.

Communication is crucial, especially in a stressful period such as this one. Learning about your service(wo)man's military mission and lifestyle will help prevent many uncertainties, misunderstandings, false expectations, and worries, especially if the service member is about to deploy to a combat environment. As the days, weeks, and months ahead can be hard for everyone involved, communication is very important and can't be stressed enough.

Despite the many who claim otherwise, the military spouse leads a different life from most. This truth becomes especially evident when our family prepares for a deployment. The time surrounding the pre-deployment phase quite often is a time of conflicting emotions as the time nears to say our good byes. A deployment is a scary and very emotional journey for both the one leaving and those left behind. During the phase of pre-deployment, the military member is working extra-long and late hours in order to ready the unit. Packing of all the necessary equipment, deployment-specific training, weapons training, and coordination with those that will be replaced in the theater of operation are only a few of the many requirements that must be met before departure. So, while we yearn to spend time together before the actual deployment, we usually see each other less due to all the preparations. This, in turn, leaves us moody and depressed, causing even more stress and anxiety within the family. And while we know that we should cherish each other and make the most of the time we have left before the departure, we tend to argue about the smallest and silliest things simply because of this heightened tension. During this phase, many families find that they often distance themselves and withdraw from each other without consciously knowing it.

While it is already very hard to figure out how to handle one's own feelings during such a trying time, the different levels of understanding of our children cause additional difficulties. While children may not always understand the specifics of the deployment, they do sense increased stress in their homes. All children react to their parent's deployment differently, which is partly influenced by their age, personality, and coping strategies.

PRE-DEPLOYMENT Phase through a child's eyes:

"Will Daddy come back?" — Age 5
"I don't want Daddy to go." — Age 7
"Will Dad have juice packs to drink?" — Age 8
"Mom and I will do everything together. — Age 14

PHASE 2: DEPLOYMENT

In the deployment phase, the unit and your service(wo)man have left the home station and are in the theater of operations performing their assigned mission.

The first couple of days are some of the most confusing and difficult to bear. The house feels empty. Those left behind feel alone. Spouses and kids anxiously await the first phone call or email from their loved ones from across the ocean. Everything seems to cause some sort of hurt as everything reminds of the long period of separation they have just begun: the freshly washed laundry that won't be in the hamper again for months to come; the boots in the corner next to the door that won't be worn again within this current season; the favorite yogurt that won't be purchased again during the next 50 or so weekly grocery runs; the pillow in bed, that won't be used for too many nights to come; the toothbrush; the monthly magazine subscriptions; the empty spot on the couch; the... everything.

This is usually the time we simply want to curl up and feel sorry for ourselves and our current situation. We're upset with the military for taking our spouse yet again. We're angry with our spouse for working for an entity that requires him or her to be separated from the family for months at a time. We're irritated with the world for being so very predisposed to conflict. We're angry about everything and everyone. In short, we can be an emotional wreck for the first couple of days, if not weeks, after our service(wo)man has left us. It's a time in which we temporarily lose ourselves, but desperately need to find ourselves again in order to make it through the months to come.

This period of feeling sorry for ourselves is usually followed by the realization that our spouse's absence does give us the opportunity to do things we didn't have or didn't take time for before. Pursuing these newly rediscovered enjoyable activities, however, may cause guilt and shame to rise within us. After all, how can we let ourselves enjoy anything while our loved one is in remote, possibly dangerous situations? Do we even have the right to try to regain some sort of normalcy within our lives while our spouses are deployed? Or does doing so automatically imply that we no longer miss or need our spouses? Throughout the process of deployment, spouses experience an array of emotions, ranging from guilt to pride, as we try to adjust to separation. We are all well aware that while our lives (have to) go on back home, our service(wo)man's life is rather put on hold for the entire duration of the deployment.

While some of us try to purposely lose track of time during a deployment, others count the days, weeks, and months that pass and the time that is still before us. A "Deployment Tracker," like the one illustrated here, is a useful way to keep track of time should you wish to as well. That way, one can mark and celebrate important milestones, such as the glorious halfway point, which in turn may give everyone involved some sort of second wind for the subsequent portion of the deployment. However, it's important to remember that this great visual device is still just an estimate, since we don't actually know when redeployment will occur.

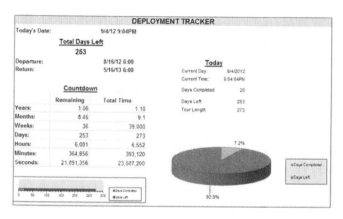

To some, being able to calculate how long one has been apart from loved ones is comforting, and they may feel their loneliness somewhat alleviated by each tally mark that can be simultaneously added to the count of days passed and subtracted from the count of days remaining. But to others, it's less comforting, as it also makes them acutely aware of the calendar, which in turn may let time appear to be stagnant. For those, ignoring the deployment clock seems to work much better in getting through this time. It doesn't matter which you choose – to count the days or ignore them - all that matters in the end is that we will reunite eventually and that every day is one day closer to homecoming.

DEPLOYMENT Phase through a child's eyes:

"Maybe if I'm really good, Santa will bring Daddy home for Christmas." —Age 5

"I want Daddy to bring me to bed!" —Age 6

"I hope Daddy has a pillow and a nice warm bed!" —Age 6

"Is Dad's being-away time over yet?" —Age 8

"Is Daddy safe over there?" —Age 10

PHASE 3: REDEPLOYMENT/DEMOBILIZATION

During this stage, preparation begins for the return. Your service member is preparing to return home and the family is preparing for the return of their service member. It's important to understand and remember that the reunion is more than just your service(wo)man coming home. It is a major event in the life of the military person, as well as his or her family. Though the anticipation of the service member's return is exciting, we usually feel some sense of apprehension and conflicting emotions. Adjustments will be required by both the service member and the family members who stayed behind.

How will he have changed? Will she notice that I gained a couple of pounds? Will he have changed physically/mentally? Will she still be attracted to me? Will we still get along? Is there still room for me in their lives? Will my son remember me? Will my daughter accept me back into her life? How will our children adjust to having their father back in their lives? Will my children still listen to me? These are just some of the issues we as a family worry about prior to redeployment. These subject matters might seem quite irrelevant and unimportant to you, but they are of real concern to us.

Part of the preparations made to return home involves a weeklong mandatory reintegration program that is meant to help both the deployee and spouse transition back into a normal life. These programs include sessions on subjects such as marital relationships, child care, and suicide awareness. The fact that the military deems such a program important and necessary enough to mandate the participation of all deployment-involved families greatly confirms and verifies how mentally taxing and difficult this homecoming-process truly is.

REDEPLOYMENT Phase through a child's eyes:

"Can I show dad to my new teacher?" —Age 6
"Will Dad play a lot with me when he gets home?" —Age 7
"How much will rules change again?" —Age 11
"Will Dad be mad about my grades?" —Age 12
"Will Dad be angry that I'm wearing make-up and dating?" —Age 16

PHASE 4: POST-DEPLOYMENT

During this phase of the deployment cycle, the service member is home readjusting to work and family life, and the family is readjusting to having their service member home. Military families call this post-deployment stage "reintegration." It's a rather emotionless term for a process fraught with emotions. And a process it is! When two people live separate lives for extended periods of time under the intensely stressful circumstances of deployments, their reunion involves much more than a tight embrace and a romantic kiss. This can be a quite difficult period for the entire family, if not the most difficult one of the whole deployment process.

What makes redeployment so difficult is that, after struggling with separation, we were finally able to normalize our drastically changed and interrupted daily lives, and now we need to reverse and rearrange it yet again in order to return to pre-deployment conditions. But why, you ask, do we need to do that? Why is any readjustment necessary? Shouldn't it be fairly easy to fall right back into where we left off (months ago)? Here, it is important to remember that during the absence of our military spouses, our lives did not stand still, but rather evolved in an attempt to live a somewhat normal life without having our service member around. While some families are able to return to their "normalcy" within a couple of days, many do not and take longer to readjust to having each other around again.

So, redeployment then essentially means letting someone who has been gone for months at a time back into our lives. Having both been independent people that whole time, going back to making joint decisions can be quite challenging. This reuniting as a family involves changes for both the serving member as well as the family. The first couple of days and weeks are usually joyous and exhilarating, as the homecoming is still very new and exciting. After all, the day our deployed service members return is the day we on the home front have been anticipating since the moment they left. But after a while, neither side can any longer deny that certain changes have occurred during this long period of separation. Time and circumstances can have a very powerful impact. People simply grow and change as time passes. Roles and responsibilities may have shifted and may never return to their previous states. For some, this phase of the deployment cycle can cause more stress than the actual deployment because of the individual and collective changes that have taken place and the uncertainty of what life will bring after such a long period of separation. Changes that occurred during the deployment will either have to be accepted or agreed upon. Both sides have to essentially teach themselves how to live together again. They need to reunite, readjust, and reconnect. They have to reintegrate into each other's lives again.

> **POST-DEPLOYMENT PHASE through a child's eyes:**
>
> "I want just Dad to take me to school." —Age 7
> "I can't wait for some me and Dad time." —Age 9
> "I've become used to just Mom and I don't want that to change" —Age 12
> "The first thing I would like to do is take a hike; just Dad and me." —Age 15
> "When will Dad have to leave again?" —All ages

COMMON MISCONCPETIONS ABOUT DEPLOYMENT

I have asked a number of people what common misconceptions regarding deployments they have encountered over the years. Here are some of their responses:

> **What some people think about deployments that are just not true:**
>
> • "What bothers me the most is people's opinion that we have no right to complain about deployments since we knew what to expect
> when we signed up for the service or became affiliated with the military. Yes, our soldiers have chosen to serve the United States. And, yes, we as spouses have chosen to support that service by marrying our soldiers. Aren't civilians glad someone has stepped up to protect their nation? After all, the alternative to the all-volunteer military is a mandatory service."
> • "Many believe that because we are military families, we can handle whatever comes our way and that we are used to separation. People really think we are superhuman, but we are not. Separation from your loved ones never gets easier!"
> • "What I find most upsetting is that people think we get tons of extra money for deployments... Yes there is extra money, but that doesn't make up for our families

being separated for such long periods and knowing our loved ones are in dangerous situations."

• "Many civilians feel the need to present their opinion about the war when they find out that my wife is deployed. The reality, however, is that I don't really care about anyone's political opinions. Don't talk about how we shouldn't be over there, and how we shouldn't be doing this   or that, while being fully aware that my spouse is putting her life on the line by doing her duty and protecting her   country. Politics are the last thing on my mind. I just want my spouse to come home safely."

• Most people automatically "can't imagine it" – meaning they think they understand the differences without even asking   or thinking about it!

• "Many people think deployed military members get time off for holidays and other important events to come home. They   believe that the deployed get to come home for important events such as the birth of their baby. The truth, however, is that many won't get to meet their new baby until s/he is a couple of weeks (sometimes even months) old."

• "I think I am the most frustrated with family saying how easy it is or will be. I know that they are only trying to   make me feel better, but I really don't want to hear it from anyone who hasn't him/herself gone through such a long and dangerous period of separation! I grant such an   opinion only to those who have experienced a deployment   first hand!"

• "People think communication is great! In reality, however, daily access to internet is not necessarily a given, and phone conversations are often marked by bad reception and delays."

• "So many civilians believe that every deployment is the same or will become easier over time, 'This is your 3rd deployment, you know what to expect by now.' The fact is, deployments DO NOT become easier, and they are NOT the same. Each deployment is hard on us, every single one. And each comes with its own unique challenges and difficulties."

• "It's the worst when others feel the need to call us to let us know that they just saw in the news that someone over there was killed. We really don't need to hear about that! We feel awful when someone over there is hurt or killed, but when we're worried about our deployed spouse, we don't need to hear that 5 Marines got killed and they don't know who they are yet."

• "I can't believe that there are still people out there that are convinced that when soldiers are told about a deployment, they can simply say 'I don't want to go,' and the military will say, 'Ok, you don't have to.' It's NOT a choice! If you're being told that you will deploy, you will have to deploy."

• "There are so many people out there that believe that once we are back from our deployments, everything goes right back to normal; that nothing has changed; that we and our loved ones pick up right where we left off. They couldn't be any more wrong!"

• "Prior to my spouse's deployment to Baghdad, a relative asked me if I was moving to Baghdad too and getting an apartment there. My response was a polite explanation that I would not be seeing him for a year, since he was going to a warzone."

• "I still can't comprehend how insensitive others can be at times. Here I am, in the middle of a long separation due to my spouse's deployment when my friend comes to tell me how she can't stand the fact that her boyfriend is out on a job for an entire week. She really doesn't know how she is going to survive this oh-so-long week... Next time you feel the need to express how much you are missing your significant other because s/he has been gone for one week, hold it back, and instead, try to imagine what it would feel like having to multiply this week, those

7 days, by 56. Get some perspective, people!"
- "I had to listen to multiple people telling me that kids don't really mind having one parent gone for a while. After all, there are plenty of other kids that only have one parent."
- "What saddens me the most is the fact that my family and friends avoid talking about the subject altogether..."

CONSEQUENCES OF WAR

A) DIVORCE

Many military families can attest that the wounds of war can easily follow a service member home. As a result, a growing number of husbands and wives are finding themselves in a new battlefield: their own homes. Deployment is a challenging time for military families. The challenge was particularly acute in the early 2000s since military families have had to face multiple deployments since September 11, 2001; each deployment requiring the relentless renegotiation of roles throughout the entire deployment process. After ten years (an entire decade) of war, separation and trauma, divorce is an unfortunate consequence shared by many military families.

According to the Pentagon, with more than 30,000 military marriages having come to an end in 2011, the military divorce rate is at its highest in ten years. The overall military divorce rate of 3.7% in 2011 edged out the most recent U.S. civilian rate of 3.5% in 2009, recorded by the Centers for Disease Control and Prevention. This divorce rate among civilians has been in decline since 2000.[25]

This percentage, however, might in actuality be even higher, as there are no numbers on military divorces that take place after a couple's permanent separation from the military. Sometimes, the couple will hold it together hoping that separation from the service will change things, but divorce ensues nonetheless. Those numbers, then, are counted toward the civilian divorce rate, even though they are more likely a result of the couple's service.

During a deployment, our service(wo)men concentrate on doing a very important job, keeping themselves and others out of harm's way, and doing whatever they need to in order to survive their deployment. Once they return, it takes a lot of give and take on both sides in order to ease the transition. Things might not be exactly like they were before or during the deployment. In fact, things will usually be different; but different is okay... Whether we are part of the civilian or military world, any marriage that aspires to be successful requires our best efforts. Sometimes it helps to remember that being married simply takes work; and that being married with extraneous stressors such as those of the military lifestyle, takes that effort required to a higher level. We are strong, but sometimes even the strong need support. Help, support, and encourage your service(wo)man and his or her family in any way possible, especially during times like these!

B) POST-TRAUMATIC STRESS DISORDER (PTSD)

Although our service member may return unharmed in the physical sense, many may experience other types of aftereffects, such as anxiety, emotional numbness, flashbacks of traumatic events, irritability, or anger. These, and more, are symptoms of Post-Traumatic Stress Disorder (PTSD).

Instances of PTSD are identified more and more in many returning service members. Some estimates suggest that 35 percent of military members returning from Iraq suffer from PTSD. As American presence in Afghanistan continues, these numbers will likely remain steady or increase.[26]

Members of the military with more than one deployment have significantly higher rates of mental health problems. With multiple tours, our modern veterans will become exponentially more vulnerable to joining the ranks of the walking wounded.[27] In fact, the psychological toll of these deployments is quite high compared with the physical injuries of combat.[28]

While the number of killed and wounded military members of previous wars, such as in Vietnam and Korea, have been much higher, casualties of a different kind (namely mental health conditions) are just beginning to be understood and considered.

Repeated deployments have unforeseen consequences. Never before in the history of warfare have we exposed our service members to such prolonged combat with little to no down time, which is much needed for decompressing overly taxed psyches.

Currently, there is no single cure for PTSD; we can only treat the symptoms. And in most cases, treatment is only initiated after the home life of a diagnosed soldier has already been drastically affected. Public awareness of this very issue is a start; and where better to start informing than among the friends and families of our military members?

DEPLOYMENT PERSPECTIVES

What follows are different perspectives of experiences service members and their families have been subjected to during deployment. The first section will illustrate the perspective of a deployed service member, and the second will present the viewpoint of someone left behind back home.

THOUGHTS OF A DEPLOYED:
(Anonymous)

"While a news network may send journalists along with the troops in order to illustrate the life of a soldier in action, they'll never actually see what it's really like through the eyes of a soldier. There is so much more to being sent to a combat zone than the actual time within that very region. When I deployed for the first time, my unit spent weeks in the field conducting training exercises followed by numerous long days fixing vehicles, replacing equipment, and preparing connexes for shipment. The little "free time" that was available was spent trying to maximize times with friends and family before the departure. I felt that every moment was precious, but at the same time the lingering deployment was always in the back of my mind. I was trying to enjoy the present, but I couldn't ignore the fact that I would be leaving for a combat zone in a couple of months. Despite this feeling of impending doom, I was also excited by the prospects of using the skills that I had spent years developing and the idea of finally being a member of the club…the club of men who populated the VFW halls. For many soldiers, the idea of going to war is the ultimate feat of manhood. I wanted to be a part of that group. I wanted to prove my value.

Unfortunately (or fortunately, depending on your perspective), deployments rarely live up to the hype. For most deployed soldiers, boredom is the predominant state. A routine rapidly evolves and most soldiers fall into a cycle of work and occasional recreation. It's hard to generalize about deployment conditions because they vary widely depending on theater, job, rank, etc. However, I think there are several common experiences and certain conditions that seem to hold true:

1. No matter how good the conditions are, they are

Spartan compared to the way most of us live back home. Even the best conditions are meager at best, and some places are simply deplorable. It's hard to stay positive when you are sharing a trailer with five other people, and it's even harder when you are sharing a tent with ten.

You start to miss those things that others back home take for granted: a real bed, a real shower, some privacy... Funny how much you start to value the very little (sometimes even seemingly unimportant) things in life when you don't have them.

2. Time to think = time to obsess about what is going on at home. Little problems become huge problems. You spend hours dwelling on the phone call or email or letter that you received from your spouse or significant other. Irrational thoughts prevail and dominate your psyche. Even the most stable marriages are called into doubt. Sometimes this condition is relieved by consistent contact home, but not everyone has that ability. Calling home from this place is probably the most precious ability to have out here. But when you only have an opportunity to call home once or twice a week, that lifeline becomes all the more important. It always feels so good to talk to my family, but it's always a bittersweet feeling. You keep hoping and waiting for a chance to call home, and if you don't get through or no one answers, you feel like crap. Hearing familiar voices on the phone feels so very good until about an hour after calling, when the homesickness sets in. You want to go to a phone and talk to them again but it's not like at home where the phone's just waiting for you. Here, a phone is usually shared by multiple people. And you don't want to hold up others who want to call their families.

3. Arrival in a deployment theater often brings with it a great deal of excitement but the excitement wears off fast.

Whether you are a combat soldier or a staff officer, the first several weeks are a blur. You feel involved and important. You feel like you are making a difference and contributing to something important. Over time, that feeling wears off and it's easy to transition into lethargy, followed by despair. Most units don't experience overwhelming success. Current operations like Iraq and Afghanistan have evolved slowly. The pace of change is discouraging and incomprehensible to most soldiers, making it difficult to stay motivated and positive. Even the most positive members of the team seem to burn out around 9-10 months. Regardless of what you do or where you work, working 15-18 hour days 7 days a week is exhausting.

4. You never know for sure when you get to come back home. You may hear rumors, but you don't want to get too excited. And even if those rumors hold to be true, the order to go home may not have you leave for another month. Nonetheless, it's still hard not to start planning on going home and to think about what you'll do once you get back. It's probably the most discussed subject down range. Once you hear rumors of redeployment, you start to wonder when you should tell your family. Should you wait until you are sure or should you tell them beforehand? How can I discuss how much I want to go home when I can't tell them that there is a possibility of it coming true soon? Is it worth having them know I'm coming home and getting their hopes up?

5. Deployments make you better at your job. Maybe it's the hours, maybe it's the scope of increased responsibility, and perhaps it's simply the pressure of the environment. Whatever it is, deployments improve your skills. My boss once said that every hour deployed is equal to three hours of work in garrison (non-deployed environment). This is certainly true. Deployed soldiers are thrust into positions

of increased responsibility and importance and most of them rise to the challenge. Returning soldiers are more confident, more competent, and more mature.

6. During a deployment, you can't help but wonder how many people back home actually remember us being over here. Once the news networks realize that ratings are on the decline, we are usually being moved back to just having the headlines reported, which then is followed by the latest story on the newest blockbuster movie. And just that quickly, the country forgets that there are thousands of people over here that have been involuntarily taken from their families. Many of our fellow countrymen forget we are at war because it simply doesn't impact their lives. Besides our families and a few of our friends, how many people really think of us? It truly seems that after the headlines have crossed the screen, Americans are distracted by the latest gossip or the new reality show.

7. Much time is filled with personal reflection and contemplation during war, as everybody here has plenty of time to think and ponder. Some might even start to question their own existence, because there's always the possibility (however small) that they may not exist much longer. Anybody who thinks they know everything about him/herself or the world would do well to be in a situation like this, as it makes you examine your own beliefs and look at them from various angles in a different light.

The experiences of a deployment will change you. Nobody comes back from a deployment the same. It's a transformative experience, both personally and professionally. You learn a lot about yourself, your family, and your friends. Not all changes are negative. For many soldiers a deployment improves self-confidence and maturity. Of course, the negative effects of combat and deployment are well documented. Many soldiers return with significant psychological problems (which are not always immediately apparent) that require months, if not years, to work out. When I returned from each of my deployments, I felt that I had significantly improved my job skills, but I was also irritable and easily annoyed. I was also angry because I felt that I had lost a significant period of my life. It took me a while to adjust back to normal life. But the experiences of a deployment will always stay with you. The things I've seen here have made me be thankful for what I have and given me a new outlook on the world.

I always have to remind myself that only a very small number of people have actually experienced the type of things I have. Not many people have been in an actual war. It's not a training exercise; it's a real war. The possibility of an imminent death is as real as the rounds in our M-16s.

I don't feel special for what I have done. I was scared every single day. I was homesick every single day. And I missed my family every single day.

Veterans have seen the other side of peace. We realize that war isn't a game or some adventure that CNN or FOX shows us highlights of. War is a tragedy, no matter what the outcome. It's the darker side of life. It's civilization at its worst. It's something that will always be around, as long as mankind exists."

THOUGHTS OF SOMEONE LEFT BEHIND:
(Anonymous)

"I wake up in the morning, knowing I won't get to see him today but that there's a fifty percent chance that I could hear from him. That's what motivates me to get up and start each day.

The news is on. The recent events are disturbing and some-what unsettling. My thoughts are consumed with his safety. I force myself not to look at the TV any longer. I've had my fill.

My laptop and cell phone have become extensions of my arms at this point. There's nothing worse than missing a call from your loved one when you know that you might not get another chance to talk to each other for a couple of days. Sometimes it's embarrassing to admit how addicted I am to those two devices, but in reality, these are the only two connections I have to my husband right now, and I miss him.

Whenever we do get to talk to each other on the phone, I continue to lie to him, tell him I am okay, when in reality, I'm breaking inside. I think the reality of it all is that we both are tired. Tired of having to say goodbye to each other, tired of being apart, tired of enduring yet another family separation. I don't need another phone call; what I need is for my family to be together again, without the next deployment lurking around the corner already.

One of the many pieces of unsolicited advice that we military wives are repeatedly told is that we indeed are lucky that our husbands aren't gone for years at a time, like the husbands from wars past, and that we ought to be aware of how fortunate we are to receive such heavily sanctioned support from the military. While this might be true, I do, however, believe that the current American military and society as a whole were entirely unprepared for the seemingly endless and repeated training and deployment cycle of today's armed forces, and the pressure and tension it puts on everyone who has ever loved a soldier.

As a military spouse, I've had to listen to the well-known cliché "absence makes the heart grow fonder" ad nauseam throughout my husband's deployment. While this response might have been extended as some sort of comfort by well-meaning people, it really just decried my current state of being at that very point in time. For me, absence really just makes my heart grow...well, lonelier.

One of the hardest parts of deployments for me is loneliness. I am expected to carry on my daily life without the one person with whom I want to share my life with. I am forced to find that delicate balance between keeping my love alive and warding off heartbreak. I miss my husband, it's that simple.

It is a very lonesome and difficult time. And while I am blessed to be surrounded by amazing friends and neighbors, my family is spread throughout the country. But even if my family were close, no one that has not experienced a deployment can understand. I love my family, but during times like these, no one will be able to understand you as well as others that have experienced the same.

A deployment is quite a learning experience. It teaches you both so much about love, life, and each other. I'm grateful for what we have and I treasure every second we have together. No matter the distance, no matter the time away, I have made a commitment and will always stand by him and support him!

Every night, I look at the picture of us on the nightstand and say 'Good night, baby. I love you. I miss you. Be safe, and come home soon.' Tomorrow is another day. Tomorrow is one day closer to him coming home."

Your love, friendship, and support have probably already been tested by your service member's decision to join the service. It was the strength of your devotion, patience, and understanding that has allowed your relationship to continue to be what it is today. A deployment, while hard on everyone involved, has the potential to strengthen your relationship. The best way to demonstrate your support and friendship to your service(wo)man is to help the spouse, partner, and close family members who are left behind. Be there when your service(wo)man can't.

7

TWO WORLDS
- For Natalie -

A smaller share of Americans currently serve in the Armed Forces than at any other given point in time since World War II. This, in turn, has led to a growing gap between people in uniform and the civilian population.[29] Due to draft laws and regulations in place decades ago, everyone in America had similar experiences regarding war, as most families had at least one individual within the Armed Forces fighting on the front lines. During those international conflicts, the entire United States seemed to represent one philosophically united military installation, joined through the commonality of having one's husband, son, brother, or father fighting in the war. Everyone was in the same boat.

Currently, however, most people outside a military installation have little to no understanding of what it means to send a loved one off to war. They don't understand the sacrifices and the fear. They are not aware of the costs of war besides the financial ones. The result is a military far less connected to the rest of society than in previous decades. This, in turn, makes the military members' ties to their families and friends – their ties with you – the more important, as those represent the only substantial connections between the civilian and military worlds.

The chapters above were meant to illustrate, as well as explicate, some of the key differences between the military and civilian worlds; differences due mainly to the nature of your service(wo)man's career choices. These differences exist primarily around our lifestyles, relocation frequencies, social development and interactions, and the lack of personal influence and control concerning other major aspects of our lives.

Coincidentally, these are also the subject matters we as military families miss the most about a civilian lifestyle: a more permanent and steady way of life that would ease the development and preservation of interpersonal relations, while also presenting us the choice and opportunity to live near our families.

The civilian world is a world that most everyone knows. There are many things about life in the civilian world that many take for granted, such as continuously seeing your children grow or being able to call one neighborhood, or one city, your true home.

Deployed military personnel often miss large portions of their families' lives. While most civilians are able to be there to witness their baby's every developmental step and milestone, someone in the military will have to miss those precious moments with their newborn, and leave for a deployment only to return to a now walking and talking toddler.

But it's not just our spouses' and kids' lives we seem to miss out on. One of the most important aspects of civilian life that a military family as a whole misses out on is regular contact with their immediate families. As a civilian, most of you are lucky enough to have your family as a part of you, with you, and around you from day to day, which in turn enables most civilian people to be able to count on their immediate and extended families' support at any given point in time.

Military families are well aware of the fact that most military parents and in-laws have a closer connection and bond with their sons, daughters, and grandchildren who live nearby. As a result, visits to the military family are rather infrequent and sporadic, as it is more difficult to accommodate a visit to a farther location, than it is to visit someone nearby. Oftentimes, it is the military family, then, that is expected to return for holidays and other events, not the least because it was them that 'left' in the first place.

Living close to one's family is considered quite a luxury for a military family, as we know that this situation may only be temporary and will come to an end faster then we'd wish for. While we yearn to be as close and connected to our parents and siblings as they are amongst each other, we simply aren't able to stay close for extended periods of time. What we are left with, then, are the phone, internet, and occasional visits in order to stay as connected as possible.

The military life is not the easiest choice a family can make, but my family has received some huge and wonderful benefits from being part of the military. We've lived outside and all over the United States and made the most of each duty station. We've been exposed to and immersed in different local cultures. There is not a state that does not have at least one of our friends living in it; friends that have become our very close extended family that is there for us when we need someone when far away from home. We also receive many direct benefits, including healthcare, education, and paid vacation time. But the military benefits we receive are a direct result of the sacrifices we make. The awareness that we opted for this life is always there – as is a strong sense of pride that we so willingly chose this very path. It is a pride well-earned, for if individuals like your service(wo)man had not voluntarily joined the military, who else would defend our country?

As long as men and women join the military for the right reasons, our armed forces will continue to fill its ranks with brave men and women who make it a great institution and the mightiest military in the world. Be proud. Embrace us.

MY VERY OWN REFLECTION

I am a typical German: I thrive on structure and routine. I'm not a big fan of change. I don't like small talk, and I only trust those that I've had the chance to know for quite a while. I like to have control over those aspects that influence my life. These characteristics of my personality don't exactly complement the unpredictable lifestyle of the military.

When I married my husband, I had no idea what I was getting myself into. His first deployment, two weeks after our wedding, was a harsh wake-up call for me. At the time, I was a nursing school student and fully integrated in my civilian life in Germany. I had few military friends, and was oblivious to any resources available to guide me in any way. I carried a heavy weight on my shoulders, and by the time my husband came back home, that weight had nearly crushed our newly formed marriage.

The end of that first deployment closely coincided with the conclusion of my husband's tour in Europe, which meant he received orders to his next duty station back in the United States. This first move as a married couple marked the beginning of many more relocations to come.

Over the course of the last 13 years, I've often wondered if I would do it all again; if I would so willingly marry into the military if I knew then what I know now. My tenure as a military spouse has changed me. I've had to endure the challenges of living on a different continent, in a different country, far from my family. I've had to postpone my own career that I so very much wished for. And I've had to bear lengthy and sometimes unexpected separations from my husband. But I've also had the exceptional opportunity to live in wonderful places, form amazing friendships, and uncover my inner strengths and passions. I've learned how to balance being flexible yet prepared and organized, venturesome yet practical and levelheaded, adaptable yet grounded and confident. I've gotten to know myself better because of all these experiences – some wonderful, some testing and challenging, but all mine – that have shaped me and helped me become the person I am today.

Everyone's life is full of challenges and stress. We all have choices to make. We can either choose to see these testing times as an opportunity for growth and self-improvement, or we can allow ourselves to become overwhelmed and victimized by our circumstances. When we decide to view a challenge or obstacle as an opportunity for growth, we are choosing a path of resiliency. For military members in particular, this choice can make all the difference in the world.

So, despite all the hardships and moments of despair, would I do it again? Absolutely. Without a doubt. In a heartbeat. Why? Because I did it all out of love for my soldier.

While most Americans are aware of the military, they don't truly understand it and the very different way of life being a part of the military entails. We might not have the power to change how a military family is perceived and understood within the entire civilian world, but this book was an attempt to help our own extended families and our very own circles of friends within the civilian world understand us and how to support their loved ones in the military.

Writing this book has been very challenging but also personally therapeutic, as it forced me to truly think about our lives within the military, and how it impacts our interactions with the rest of our non-military family members and our civilian friends.

I've learned a lot about our lives and myself during the process of writing this book. I've come to learn to appreciate even more what our lifestyle has been offering us over the years, and it has helped me comprehend and truly understand the importance of our military community. But it has also reinforced the initial reasoning and motivation that caused me to write this book in the first place: the desire and need of our civilian friends and families to understand the military lifestyle a bit better in order to stay connected and close to each other. 13 years I have been part of this huge military family now, which constitutes a substantial portion of my time on this earth. As our lives are so different, for the majority of this time I've felt misunderstood by my own civilian family and friends. It is my hope that with this book I was able to bridge this gap between our two worlds, or at the very least initiate a starting point and desire to do so. Stay close to your service(wo)man and his or her family, for they truly need you.

SHARE THIS BOOK!

Please visit *www.UnderstandingYourServiceman.com* or *www.Facebook.com/UnderstandingYourServiceman* and share your copy of this book in order to help promote understanding between the military and civilian worlds.

After all, we all ought to know more about those who protect us.

RELATED RESOURCES

[Disclaimer: I cannot personally endorse any of these websites, books, or organizations. I am not a mental health, legal, or financial professional. Please use these sources for information only and consult professionals as necessary.]

A Family's Guide To The Military For Dummies: This comprehensive guide covers such key topics as introducing military life to readers new to the armed forces, financial planning, relocation, deployment, raising kids alone while a partner is away, and taking advantage of the available benefits. It offers tips and advice for dealing with emotions that surround events like deployments, deciphering the acronyms used in daily military life, forming support groups, keeping track of a loved one's whereabouts, and surviving on a military base in a foreign country. You can read an excerpt of the book by visiting *http://media.wiley.com/product_data/excerpt/75/04703869/04 70386975.pdf*

A Handbook For Family & Friends Of Service Members: This is a wonderful resource helping you as family and friends to understand what to expect from a deployment, how to build the skills to strengthen or repair your relationships, and how to gain the tools to keep your family and personal community strong throughout the duration of your separation.

http://www.pbs.org/thisemotionallife/sites/default/files/attachment s/2011/MFHB_PDF_Sample.pdf

CinCHouse.com: The Internet's largest community of military wives and women in uniform includes military girlfriends, fiancées, mothers, wives, and sisters. It provides timely information, and resources pertaining to military life.

https://www.cinchouse.com/

Married To The Army: A site designed specifically for new Army wives or Army parents.

http://marriedtothearmy.com/new-army-parents-guide/

Mom's Field Guide: When author Sandy Doell's son was deployed to Iraq in 2004, she felt overwhelmed with fear and anxiety. She couldn't help but worry. To keep herself busy, she turned her energies toward finding ways to support her son from the home front. After thousands of hours of research and her own first-hand experience along with many lessons she learned from other military families, she wrote Mom's Field Guide: What You Need to Know to Make It Through Your Loved One's Military Deployment. She shares what she learned with other families in the same situation. You can read more about the book by visiting

www.momsfieldguide.com

National Military Family Association: An organization that services members and their families with insightful recommendations, innovative programs, and grassroots efforts to better the quality of life for military families.

http://www.militaryfamily.org/

Not Your Average Widow: This very helpful site provides a list of websites, articles, books, organizations, and other resources for widows.
http://www.notyouraveragewidow.com/resources/

U.S. Army Deployment Cycle Readiness: Soldier's And Family Member's Handbook: This handbook is designed to be used by Soldiers and Family Members in the Active, Guard, and Reserve Components. It helps Families *"gear up"* for the various stages within the deployment cycle, providing tips, ideas, and resources that can be used.
http://wisconsinmilitary.org/wp-content/uploads/2011/12/OPREADY_DCS_Handbook.pdf

TheDirectionDiva.com: The Direction Diva is a personal blog written and edited by Judy Davis. Additionally it is a website that sells products and services that are a fit for military wives, busy moms, and women who work from home.
http://thedirectiondiva.com/

Your Soldier, Your Army: A very good survival guide to help parents cope with war and other deployments.
http://ra.defense.gov/documents/family/YourSoldier.pdf

ENDNOTES

[1]
Baker, A. (2008). *Life In The U.S. Armed Forces*. Praeger.

[2]
Hurt, A., Ryan, E., & Straley, J. (2011, July 03). By The Numbers: Today's Military. (2011). Retrieved June 21, 2012, from
http://www.npr.org/2011/07/03/137536111/by-the-numbers-todays-military

[3]
Department of the Army. (2010). Commissioned Officer Professional Development and Career Management. *DA PAM 600–3*. Retrieved from
http://www.apd.army.mil/pdffiles/p600_3.pdf

[4]
U.S. Census Bureau. (2010). *Geographical Mobility in the Past year by Age for Current Residence in the United States*. Retrieved from
http://factfinder2.census.gov/faces/tableservices/jsf/pages/productvi ew.xhtml?pid=ACS_10_1YR_B07001&prodType=table

[5]
Dawson, J. (2004). Keep Your Sanity At Moving Time: Relocation Advice for Military Families. Retrieved July 05, 2012, from
http://www.militarymoney.com/MilitaryLife/Relocation/tabid/114/itemId/2340/Default.aspx

[6]
Clearing And PCS. (2005). Retrieved July 06, 2012, from
http://militarygear.com/asp/2005/10/30/clearing-and-pcs/

[7]
Stars And Stripes. (n.d.). Managing Your Household Goods Move. Retrieved from
http://www.stripes.com/polopoly_fs/1.132791!/menu/standard/file/Managing%20Your%20Household%20Goods%20Move.pdf

[8]
Murdock, S. (n.d.). Home Is Where The Military Sends You - Getting To Know Your New Military Town. Retrieved July 12, 2012, from
http://www.militarymoney.com/MilitaryLife/Relocation/tabid/114/itemId/2339/Default.aspx

[9]
Department of Defense. (1997). Fulfilling the Military Service Obligation. *DODI 1304.25*. Retrieved from
http://www.dtic.mil/whs/directives/corres/pdf/130425p.pdf

[10]
Department of the Army. (2009). Officer Active Duty Obligation. *Army Regulation 350-100*. Retrieved from
http://www.apd.army.mil/pdffiles/r350_100.pdf

[11]
Garrett, S., & Hoppin, S. (2009). Living Life As A Military Spouse. In *A Family's Guide To The Military for Dummies*.

Retrieved from
*http://media.wiley.com/product_data/excerpt/75/04703869/04
7   0386975.pdf*

[12]
Rothman, J. (2011). America's New Military Culture.
Retrieved June 13, 2012, from
*http://articles.boston.com/2011-09-
14/bostonglobe/30155869_1_military-values-american-military-
culture-civil-society/3*

[13]
A Day In The Life Of A Military Officer. (n.d.). Retrieved
June 23, 2012, from
http://www.princetonreview.com/careers.aspx?cid=96

[14]
Steen, J., & Asaro, M. (2006). The Ultimate Sacrifice. In
Military   Widow: A   Survival   Guide. Retrieved   from
*http://books.google.com/books?id=gDVMStqyYIMC&printsec=
frontcover&dq=military+widow:+a+survival+guide#v=onepage&
q=military%20widow%3A%20a%20survival%20guide&f=false*

[15]
Davis,   T.   (n.d.).   Retrieved   June   15,   2012,   from
http://americanwidowproject.org/mission/

[16]
Steen, J., & Asaro, M. (2006). Who Is The Military Widow?
In *Military Widow: A Survival Guide*. Retrieved from
*http://books.google.com/books?id=gDVMStqyYIMC&printsec=
frontcover&dq=military+widow:+a+survival+guide#v=onepage&
q=military%20widow%3A%20a%20survival%20guide&f=false*

[17]
Insight For Families And Friends [Review of the book
Military Widow: A Survival Guide]. Retrieved June 14, 2012,

from
http://www.militarywidow.com/survival-guides/families-and-friends/

[18]
Spyrou, S. (2007). Handling Life As A Foreign-Born Military Spouse. Retrieved July 22, 2012, from
http://voices.yahoo.com/handling-life-as-foreign-born-military-spouse-686254.html?cat=41

[19]
Adjusting To The United States. (n.d.). Retrieved June 14, 2012, from
http://www.rapidimmigration.com/1_eng_coming_adjusting.html

[20]
Military Life 101. (n.d.). Retrieved July 18, 2012, from
https://www.militarykidsconnect.org/educators/militarylife101

[21]
Garrett, S., & Hoppin, S. (2009). Raising A Family In The Military. In *A Family's Guide To The Military for Dummies.* Retrieved from
http://books.google.com/books?id=qAfYUYXsc3UC&printsec=frontcover&dq=a+family%27s+guide+to+the+military&source=bl&ots=q55M5CYTog&sig=i28z10LunvHNHpWajdfFnTxNOPw&hl=en&sa=X&ei=yDlJUP2NHouc8gSNgoH4Aw&ved=0CDIQ6AEwAA#v=onepage&q=a%20family%27s%20guide%20to%20the%20military&f=false

[22]
Community. (2008). In *New World Encyclopedia.* Retrieved July 23, 2012, from
http://www.newworldencyclopedia.org/entry/Community

[23]
Casey, S. (2010). 2010 Military Family Lifestyle Survey.

Retrieved July 23, 2012, from
*http://bluestarfam.s3.amazonaws.com/42/58/2/301/2010bsfsu
rveyexecsummary.pdf*

[24]
Department of Defense. (2008). This U.S. Army
Deployment Cycle Readiness: Soldier's and Family
Member's Handbook. Retrieved August 05, 2012, from
*http://wisconsinmilitary.org/wpcontent/uploads/2011/12/OPR
EADY_DCS_Handbook.pdf*

[25]
Zoroya, G. (2011). Military Divorce Rate At Highest Level
Since 1999. *USA Today*. Retrieved from
*http://www.usatoday.com/news/military/story/2011-12-
13/military-divorce-rate-increases/51888872/1*

[26]
Institute for Operations Research and the Management
Sciences (2009, September 15). Iraq Troops' PTSD Rate
As High As 35 Percent, Analysis Finds. *ScienceDaily*.
Retrieved August 06, 2012, from
*http://www.sciencedaily.com-
/releases/2009/09/090914151629.htm*

[27]
Department of Defense. (2008). Operation Enduring
Freedom 8 Afghanistan. Retrieved August 14, 2012, from
*http://www.armymedicine.army.mil/reports/mhat/mhat_v/Redact
ed1-MHATV-OIF-4-FEB-2008Report.pdf*

[28]
Tanielian, T., Jaycox, L., & Schell, T. (2008). *Invisible
Wounds of War*. Retrieved August 16, 2012, from
*http://www.rand.org/pubs/monographs/2008/RAND_MG720
.1.pdf*

[29]

Tavernise, S. (November 24, 2011). As Fewer Americans Serve, Growing Gap Is Found Between Civilians And Military. *The New York Times*. Retrieved August 18, 2011, from

http://www.nytimes.com/2011/11/25/us/civilian-military-gap-grows-as-fewer-americans-serve.html?_r=1

23737699R10067

Made in the USA
Charleston, SC
04 November 2013